Brazilian Cooking

Brazilian Cooking

Carla Barboza Pinto

CHARTWELL
BOOKS, INC.

DEDICATION

To my mother, Maria Amélia, for sharing her recipes—secret and guarded for so long—with me, and to my father, Raul, who had to learn the hard way but who is now a Babette in his own right.

A QUINTET BOOK

Published by Chartwell Books
A Division of Book Sales, Inc.
114, Northfield Avenue
Edison, New Jersey 08837

This edition was produced for sale in the U.S.A.,
its territories and dependencies only.

ISBN 0-7858-0888-4

This book was designed and produced by
Quintet Publishing Limited
6 Blundell Street
London N7 9BH

Creative Director: Richard Dewing
Art Director: Silke Braun
Designer: Norma Martin
Senior Editor: Sally Green
Editor: Rosie Hankin
Photographer: Ferguson Hill
Food Stylist: Emma Patmore

Typeset in Great Britain by
Central Southern Typesetters, Eastbourne
Manufactured in Singapore by
Universal Graphics Pte Ltd
Printed in Singapore by
Star Standard Industries (Pte) Ltd

WARNING

Because of the risk of salmonella poisoning, raw or lightly cooked eggs
should be avoided by the elderly, the young, babies, pregnant women,
and those with an impaired immune system.

14.95

Contents

Introduction

The recipes in this book have been chosen for being typical and authentic, with the proviso that the ingredients are readily available outside Brazil. Two main influences predominate in Brazilian cuisine: first, the indigenous native Indian population, who used many techniques and ingredients in food preparation which survive today, and second, the black slaves, who brought with them a rich African contribution. These strong central influences were brought into the cuisine of the Portuguese colonizers, which was itself colored by the occupation of the Moors from North Africa. All this combined to produce an exotic and exuberant cuisine into which other Europeans in Brazil (English, Spanish, Italians, and Germans) have further mingled their own tastes and styles as Brazilian society has evolved.

Historical Context

Some say the Portuguese "discovery" of Brazil was a historical accident, the Portuguese ships having drifted off course *en route* to India. More plausible explanations exist, including that the Portuguese, better funded than their Spanish counterparts in 1500, intended to chart this new voyage to an undiscovered and—as they later found—vast and geographically diverse land.

The first large influxes of black slaves began from 1550. They came from Western Africa and brought with them tribal languages and music, with heavy drumming and dancing to accompany religious ceremonies. Three hundred years of slavery resulted in adaptations to their tribal cuisine, and the presence of slaves inside the colonist planters' homes influenced the food habits of the white masters too.

It is estimated that from 1550 through 1888 about 3½ million slaves were shipped to Brazil. A few got away. For example, in 1597 forty Africans escaped from a sugar plantation and fled to the forest, forming their own settlement of mocambos, or communities, groups of which came together and were called quilombos. For more than a century these groups thrived, going back to their culinary and religious roots, and leaving their own mark on the national cuisine.

Above: Praça Tiradentes in Ouro Prêto, Southeast Brazil.

Above: A stunning backdrop to the rooftops in Southeast Brazil.

The mid 1800s saw the growth of the bourgeoisie in Brazil and further international influences affected the cuisine. Brazil eventually outlawed slavery, but not until some fifty years after it was abolished in the US and Britain. In Brazil, as in the US, integration of black people was a slow process. Some battles were fought at the culinary front-line, when the "sweet wars" were waged on the back streets of Bahia, where former slave women fought with Portuguese housewives for the bigger market share in cocadas, acarajés, amalás, and apetês. The blacks won, their delicacies and tempting spices defeating the poorer counterparts of their white sisters.

Religion

Unlike slaves in the US, Brazilian negroes often came from Muslim backgrounds, and it was a group of Muslims who led important revolts in the northeast for religious freedom and an end to slavery. But it was the tribal practices of the Yoruba peoples which had the greater influence on Brazilian religious practices. A fascinating religious *mélange* emerged, with Yoruba deities, or Orixás, being "twinned" with Christian saints. All twelve Orixás have their own culinary favorite. (For example, Lemanjá, goddess of the waters, loves acarajés; Oxalá does not like foods with dendê and likes acaça; Ogum likes feijoada; Xangô, god of the thunder, likes amalá; and Oxum likes xinxim de galinha.) The resulting candomblé religion involved celebrations for particular gods where their favorite food would be shared among the revelers, animals were often sacrificed and would be washed down with potent cachaça-based drinks. Each September Bahians celebrate the month of the "Ibejes" twin deities Cosme and Damiao, where many dendê-based dishes were prepared. Examples include efó, xinxim, and moquecas.

Black slaves had more freedom to cook in their way if they lived away from the colonial household in the senzalas. These houses were used by large groups of plantation slaves living as communities, though with little cultural freedom. Then came the quilombos, with a strong resurgence of cultural and religious practices. Together, the senzalas and quilombos formed the basis for most of the religious, cultural, and culinary traditions of black Brazil that exist today.

The Food

There were about three million Indians in Brazil when the Portuguese came. They were already cooking with cassava and other root vegetables, eating corn and potatoes, heart of palm, turtle meat and eggs, nuts, forest fruits, and fish caught in the waters of the Amazon. They used herbs to cook with, molasses to sweeten dishes, and Malagueta peppers to give their food a kick. They used dried fish tongues to grate their guarana sticks and served food in banana leaves. The classic Brazilian fish stew, moqueca

Above: The magnificent Opera House, Manaus, Amazon, Brazil.

(see page 32), draws heavily on traditional Indian methods and ingredients.

African cooking brought even more spices but in some ways their techniques and flavors resembled the Indian methods. Their way of life dictated many of their methods. For hard plantation work, heavy bean-based dishes were used, with one batch stretching for days or weeks by constant recooking with water added each time. The Africans used different implements too, such as *pedra de ralar*, stones for grinding dried foods like shrimp into a powder for use in all sorts of dishes and sauces. Unlike the Indians, Africans cooked with oil, predominantly red palm (or dendê) oil, whereas the Indians never fried, mainly boiling and steaming their food instead.

The economy's reliance on sugar ended in the mid-nineteenth century, and other crops took sugar's place, with cotton, cocoa, corn, and coffee predominating. Following the abolition of slavery, Brazil opened her doors to all comers, and a new migrant population came to work the fields and enjoy the boom that followed the explosion of the coffee trade. Needing labor desperately to reap the full rewards, landowners paid Swiss and German economic refugee families to work the land and many became wealthy tenant farmers. Blond, blue-eyed Brazilians of German extraction are a frequent sight in Brazil, especially in the south. Italians also abounded at this time, bringing

vital know-how in manufacturing and engineering from the recession in Europe. The European immigrants brought a further layer to the already exotically mixed national style of cooking.

Brazilian food today is a combination of this vast array of diverse cultures, people, and techniques, so no wonder it is so richly satisfying and good to eat. The obvious enthusiasm of my non-Brazilian friends when I treat them to a feijoada on a cold winter's day is testament to the exportability of my country's cuisine. And on many a summer's day I have seen Brazilians and other nationalities brought closer over cachaça-soaked barbecues, marveling over my mother's secret marinades.

Specialty Ingredients

In Brazilian cookery, a few ingredients require soaking in advance. A good tip is to do the soaking in a large bowl and place it by the sink. This way, every time you pass by your kitchen sink you can either change the water or check on it.

Banana leaves

Sometimes these can be found in African, Asian, or Latin American markets. If you really like tropical food, you can buy a little banana tree. It is very pretty. Anyway, whenever using banana leaves, steam them or boil them very, very quickly, so they become softer.

Beans

All dried beans require soaking, ideally overnight, but it can be done around five or six hours before cooking. Chinese black beans are generally small and should be avoided, as should black kidney beans. Spanish delicatessens normally stock black beans from Asturias which are very good.

Cachaça/pinga

Cachaça/pinga is a spirit made from sugar cane. It is very similar to rum, but it is obtained through a further distillation process. Because of this, cachaça/pinga has a much higher alcoholic content than rum. It is considered the Brazilian national drink and Caipirinha (page 124) and Cachaça Cocktail (page 126) are prepared with it. The liquid of cachaça/pinga is normally transparent like vodka, but there is also a better quality, yellowish version, which is aged in oak barrels and can be drunk pure.

Cassava (yuca)
Cassava root and cassava flour (manioc or yuca)

In Brazil, cassava has several different names. In some north eastern states it is known as Macaxeira, in the south aipim and mandioca. Cassava (*Manihot utilissima*) is a root/tuber with a firm, dark skin. It is very starchy, and used all over Brazil. Cassava, or tapioca, flour is made from the root.

Cassava was first processed and introduced into the cuisine by the Brazilian native Indians. These people either transformed it into a liquid (Tucupi) or into different kinds of flour (cassava flour or tapioca). The root-tuber can be found in Latin, African, and West Indian specialty shops, while the flour is available from Portuguese, Spanish,

and Brazilian delicatessens.

In this book, the only recipes that use cassava root are Sweet Cassava Fries (page 15), Cream of Cassava, Shrimps Bahia-style (page 44), and Cassava Cake (page 121). All the other recipes call for cassava flour.

Coconut milk

Both thick and thin coconut milk is used in Brazilian cooking. Pour out the juice from the coconut and reserve. Run a sharp knife between the coconut meat and the outer, hard skin. (If you warm the coconut up a bit in the oven, the meat will come out more easily.) Shred the coconut flesh, and mix in a blender or food processor with its own juice. Place it in a cheesecloth and squeeze. You will be left with the thick coconut milk.

For thin coconut milk, add two cups of hot water to the previously squeezed coconut pulp. Repeat the process with the cheesecloth. You will be left with thin coconut milk.

If you can't find fresh coconuts, use canned coconut milk or shredded coconut. Put 2 cups of shredded coconut into a bowl and add 2½ cups of hot water. Let cool, then knead with your hands. Strain through a cheesecloth. Repeat the process a second time, and you will have thin coconut milk.

Cornflour—Farinha de Milho

Cornflour is a staple ingredient of many Brazilian recipes.

Dendê oil (red palm oil)

Look out for dendê oil in Brazilian specialty shops, or try West Indian and African markets. Sometimes supermarkets stock it. All the amounts of dendê oil in my recipes for Bahian dishes have been reduced by half. This is because dendê oil is quite strong and whereas Bahians are brought up on it, Brazilians who are not from the northeast would naturally generally approach it with caution when they are cooking with it.

Above: Harbor, Jericoacoara, Northeast Brazil.

Dried shrimp

See page 12.

Hearts of palm

Also frequently used as a salad vegetable.

Limes

In Brazil, there are no lemons. It is very easy today to find limes however. Use them, because they will give a more authentic flavor.

Preserved peppers

For Malagueta peppers, you should visit Brazilian specialty shops, or, occasionally, Portuguese shops. They will be preserved in vinegar or cachaça, never fresh. As a substitute, you could use chiles.

Salted cod

Wash the pieces of *bacalhau* under running water and soak overnight. Then, the following day, throw away the water, put the *bacalhau* pieces into a saucepan, cover with fresh water, bring to a boil, and simmer for about 15 to 20 minutes. Drain, remove the skin, and flake the fish. If you flake the *bacalhau* with your hands, it will be much easier to feel the bones.

Salt cod is easily available in Portuguese shops, West Indian and African markets, and sometimes in the supermarkets. The belly parts are preferable because they have more meat. Ask the shop assistant to cut it into smaller pieces, so it will be easier to soak and fit into the saucepan. When reconstituting salt cod, remember that a lot of weight will be lost from the bones, skin, and salt. Two lb of dried salt cod produces 14 oz of cooked, skinned, boneless cod.

Smoked and dried meats

All smoked and dried meats found in this book require soaking. Do change the water a few times during soaking and blanch the meat for 10 minutes to remove the salt and reconstitute.

Usually only Brazilian specialty shops stock these meats. Otherwise use alternatives. For slab bacon, you can try Italian pancetta; for sausages, use Portuguese and Spanish types—Spanish chorizos have more paprika in them.

Marinade for Meat, Poultry, and Fish

— Vinha D'alhos —

This is an old and traditional way of marinating meats, poultry, and fish. The name is so ancient that the majority of people in Brazil would not understand it any more, even though they all use it. The recipe dates back to my granny's recipes and my mother hardly cooks a dish without it. In fact, she never cooks anything with ready-made seasoning. You might think there is too much garlic in this recipe, but after cooking the garlic acquires a very distinctive flavor. Try it!

Preparation time:
5 minutes
Marinating time:
Meat and poultry: 12 hours or overnight
Fish: around 2 hours

- ◇ salt
- ◇ 5–6 garlic cloves, crushed
- ◇ Juice of 2 limes, or more depending on the amount of meat
- ◇ Ground black pepper
- ◇ Wine (for pork meat you may use vinegar)

1 With your hands, salt the meat or fish, rubbing the salt well into the flesh.

2 Mix the remaining ingredients together, and rub over the meat or fish.

3 Set aside, covered, in a cool place.

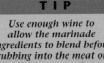

TIP

Use enough wine to allow the marinade ingredients to blend before rubbing into the meat or fish. You may use vinegar for pork instead, if you wish.

Above: A sun-drenched colonnade in Recife, Northeast Brazil.

Above: Carnival fun in Olinda, on Brazil's Northeastern coast.

Dried Shrimp

Camarão Seco

Dried smoked shrimp are frequently used in Bahia. They are sometimes available in Chinese supermarkets but, as they do not contain dendê oil, they do not taste authentic. This recipe provides a good approximation of the genuine shrimp.

*Preparation time:
20 minutes
Cooking time: 30 minutes*

- ½ lb very small, fresh shrimp, skin and heads intact
- Dendê (red palm) oil
- Salt

1 Preheat a 475°F oven. Wash and pat dry the shrimp.

2 Place them on a baking sheet. Pour ⅓ teaspoon of dendê oil over each shrimp, then sprinkle with salt.

3 Bake in the oven for about 25 minutes. Halfway through the baking time, turn them over. Keep an eye on them so they do not burn. Remove from heat.

4 If they are still oily, place them one by one on paper towels. Then heat a frying pan and heat them up again, without frying.

5 Let cool and use them in recipes that require ground, dried shrimp.

TIP

The smaller the shrimp, the better the result. The only exception is acarajé, which requires larger shrimp.

Appetizers

Fried Salt Codfish Cakes

Sweet Cassava Fries

Fried Black-eyed Pea Cakes

Bite-size Cheese Bread

Fried Rice Cakes

Apples Filled with Shrimp Cream

Water Cress and Heart of Palm Salad

Heart of Palm Dip

Crab in its Shell

Filled Bread Loaf

Langoustine Gratin in Pineapple Shell

Lebanese-style Baked Cakes

Cheese and Bean Soup

Shredded Kale Soup

Fried Salt Codfish Cakes

Bolinho de Bacalhau

These cakes are sold everywhere. They are the perfect accompaniment to a cold beer at the bar. Because they are so light, you can easily eat dozens of them.

Serves 4

Preparation time: 1½ hours, excluding soaking
Cooking time: 15 minutes

- ⋄ 9 oz potatoes, peeled and cubed
- ⋄ 1½ lb salted cod, reconstituted (see page 10)
- ⋄ Generous bunch of fresh parsley, chopped
- ⋄ 1 onion, chopped
- ⋄ 1 garlic clove, chopped
- ⋄ Salt and ground black pepper
- ⋄ 2 eggs
- ⋄ Oil, for deep frying

1 In a large saucepan, boil the potatoes until soft. What you really want is a hard mash consistency. Let cool well.

2 Cook the salted cod for around 15 minutes. Strain and skin the fish. Then shred it with your hands so you can look out for bones. Whisk in a blender or food processor, or pass through a meat mincer.

3 When the potatoes have cooled, in a large mixing bowl, put the parsley, onions, and garlic, the cod, some pepper and taste for salt. Salted cod always retains some salt, even after the preparation, so be cautious. Add the eggs, then mix well.

4 Make small balls the size of a plum, or shape them like little spring rolls, and leave to rest on baking sheets in the refrigerator for one hour before frying.

5 Heat the oil to 350 to 360°F in a saucepan. Fry a few balls at a time, turning them upside-down when slightly golden. Remove with a slotted spoon and place on paper towels. Serve them with Malagueta pepper sauce (see page 41), or any tomato relish, or on their own.

Picturesque building façades, Salvador, Northeastern coast of Brazil.

Sweet Cassava Fries
Mandioquinha Frita

In Brazil, cassava fries are as common as French fries. All bars and pubs will have them on their snack menu. They are delicious with a very cold beer.

Serves 4

Preparation time:
15 minutes
Cooking time:
30–35 minutes
Frying time: 15 minutes

- 1½ lb cassava root, peeled and halved
- Salt, generous pinch of
- Water
- Vegetable oil, for deep frying

1 Cut the cassava root into 3-inch round pieces, then cut them in half again.

2 Put the cassava pieces into a large saucepan, add water to come halfway up the vegetables and add salt.

3 Bring to a boil and cook over medium heat for about 30 to 35 minutes, until soft. Drain well.

4 Using a small knife, cut into strips like French fries.

5 Heat the oil well and fry them until golden, turning them over once. Remove with a slotted spoon and place onto paper towels.

6 Add more salt and serve hot with a tomato relish to serve as a dip.

Fried Black-eyed Pea Cakes

Acarajé

Acarajé is one of the most famous Bahian appetizers. There is a variation of Acarajé called Amalá, when a tablespoon of dendê oil is added to the mixture. Amalá is wrapped in bananas and steamed.

Makes 20 cakes

Preparation time: 20 minutes (excluding soaking)
Frying time: 20 minutes

- 1⅓ cups black-eyed peas
- 1 large onion, chopped
- Salt
- White pepper, to taste
- 2 pods preserved Malagueta pepper, drained and mashed with a fork, or

- ½ teaspoon any Caribbean hot pepper sauce
- ½ cup dendê oil
- Vegetable oil, for frying
- 20 small dried shrimp
- One-third quantity Vatapá (see page 31)

TIP

Brazilians from Bahia would fry the cakes in pure dendê oil, but this can be quite strongly flavored, especially if you are not used to it. Mixing the frying oils is the best alternative as it still gives an authentic touch to your recipe.

1 Like all varieties of beans, black-eyed peas need to be soaked before cooking. As they are not precooked in the preparation of this recipe, you should allow them to soak for 24 hours. Every so often squeeze the peas in their soaking water and rub them together a few times, to help soften the skins. Each time you do this, throw the water away, and cover once more with fresh water. The skins will rise to the surface. Using a slotted spoon, remove the skins and drain the peas once they are completely soaked.

2 Now place the peas into a blender or food processor, and blend until they reach a coarse consistency. Add the chopped onion to the mixture but do not blend again as the onion would make the mixture too soft and the cakes would fall apart while frying.

3 Using a wooden spoon, mix in salt, white pepper, and the mashed Malagueta peppers or pepper sauce. Now using two metal spoons, scoop up small amounts of the mixture and form little cakes, the size of a smallish lime. Place the cakes on waxed paper, and add to each one a dried shrimp, burying them halfway but without covering them totally.

4 In a heavy, deep saucepan, combine the dendê oil with vegetable oil, enough to cover three-quarters of the cakes. Heat the oil to 350°F. Cook for about 5 minutes, starting shrimp side down, in batches of four or five. Turn occasionally to cook evenly.

5 With a slotted spoon, remove the cakes from the heat, and place them on paper towels to drain. Keep them warm in the oven.

6 To serve, cut the cakes partially lengthwise and fill with a little vatapá. Otherwise use a tiny amount of Malagueta sauce (see page 41) or acarajé sauce.

Bite-size Cheese Bread
— Pão de Queijo —

These cheese balls are very popular in Minas Gerais, São Paulo, and Rio. They were probably invented in Minas, a state traditionally renowned for its dairy products. Today they are found all over several Brazilian states, in malls and airports, and everywhere you find small huts called Pão de Queijo houses. Pão de Queijo is made with polvilho azedo, which is very fine, sour cassava flour. It can be found in most Brazilian stores and occasionally in Portuguese ones.

Makes 20 rolls

Preparation time:
20 minutes
Cooking time: 20 minutes

- ⋄ 1 cup polvilho azedo
- ⋄ ¾ cup flour
- ⋄ 1 teaspoon salt

- ⋄ ⅓ teaspoon dried yeast or baking powder
- ⋄ ½ cup finely and freshly grated Parmesan cheese
- ⋄ ½ cup warm milk
- ⋄ 3 Tbsp butter
- ⋄ 2 eggs, beaten

1 Preheat a 375°F oven. Into a large mixing bowl, sift the polvilho azedo and the flour. Add the salt, yeast or baking powder, and Parmesan cheese. Mix gently.

2 Warm the milk, but do not boil. Add the butter, wait until melted, then pour the liquid into the mixing bowl with the dry ingredients. Add the beaten eggs. Mix well, but gently. Cover the bowl and let stand by the warm oven for 30 minutes.

3 Form small balls of dough the size of a fresh date and place them on a baking sheet. Place on top of a flat cake pan in the oven and bake for 20 minutes. Serve hot.

Right: Bite-size Cheese Bread

Fried Rice Cakes
— Bolinho de Arroz —

In Brazil, we eat rice and beans nearly every day. Therefore, we normally have lots of rice and beans left. This recipe is normally prepared to use up leftovers of rice.

Serves 4–6

Preparation time:
20 minutes
Cooking time: 15 minutes

- ⋄ ½ cup milk
- ⋄ 1 tsp baking powder
- ⋄ 1 tsp sugar
- ⋄ 2 cups cooked rice
- ⋄ 2 eggs, beaten
- ⋄ Salt

- ⋄ 2 Tbsp flour
- ⋄ Chopped fresh parsley
- ⋄ Oil, for deep frying

TIP

These cakes also taste delicious if you add half a sliced banana to the original mixture before forming the cakes and frying them.

1 In a large bowl, add the baking powder and sugar to the milk, stirring to dissolve.

2 Add the rice, the eggs, and a little salt. Little by little add the flour and the parsley. Keep on stirring until you reach a smooth consistency.

3 Roll little cakes the size of plums, and fry them, in very hot oil, until golden. Place on paper towels.

4 Eat hot or cold. When eating cold, make a little mixture of sugar and cinnamon and dip the cakes in it.

Apples filled with Shrimp Cream

Maçãs Recheadas com Crème de Camarão

*This is a good starter, which can be prepared in advance—you can bake the apples just before serving.
To prevent the apples darkening, sprinkle them with a little lemon juice.*

Serves 6

*Preparation time:
20 minutes
Cooking time: 45 minutes*

- 6 cooking apples, such as Baldwin, Cortland, or Northern Spy
- 2 Tbsp vegetable or olive oil

- 1 onion, shredded
- 9 oz shrimp, fresh or frozen
- 2 fresh plum tomatoes, peeled and chopped
- Salt and ground black pepper
- 1 Tbsp butter
- 2 Tbsp flour
- 2½ cups milk

1 Polish the apples well with a dry cloth. With a small knife, cut the tops off and reserve. With a teaspoon, scoop out the insides.

2 Heat the oil in a frying pan. Fry onions and shrimp for 5 minutes. Add tomatoes, salt, and pepper.

3 Preheat a 325°F oven. In another small saucepan, melt the butter over low heat. Add the flour, stirring continuously. When blended, add the milk little by little. Stir over the heat until you reach a white sauce consistency, then pour into the shrimp mixture.

4 Fill the apples with the shrimp cream, reserving some for pouring round. Put the tops back on the apples.

5 Butter an ovenproof dish. Place the apples into it side by side. Pour the remaining sauce around the apples. Bake in the oven for 25 minutes.

Watercress and Heart of Palm Salad

Salada de Agrião e Palmito

Heart of palm is extracted from inside the palm tree trunk. It is easy to find, canned in supermarkets. In Brazil you need to shop around for a soft, tender Palmito, while elsewhere there is no need—the best South American Palmito is exported.

Serves 4

Preparation time: 20 minutes

- 10½ oz washed watercress or young spinach leaves
- 1 lb canned heart of palm
- 16 ripe cherry tomatoes
- 1 yellow bell pepper, roasted, peeled, and cut into strips
- 12 quail eggs, hard-cooked or 2–3 small hard-cooked eggs
- 3 Tbsp chopped fresh parsley

For the dressing
- 9 Tbsp olive oil
- 3 Tbsp white wine vinegar
- 1 garlic clove, crushed (optional)
- Salt and ground black pepper

1 Chop the watercress. Drain the heart of palm sticks and slice them into 1-inch pieces.

2 Put the watercress into a salad bowl with the tomatoes and yellow bell pepper. Toss well.

3 Peel the quail eggs and cut them in half lengthwise. Scatter the eggs and heart of palm slices into the salad bowl and add the chopped parsley.

4 Mix the dressing ingredients together with salt and pepper to taste. Dress the salad just before serving.

Heart of Palm Dip
Paté de Palmito

Use this dip for raw carrot sticks, celery, and cauliflower, or any other raw vegetable.
In Brazil, we normally prepare it with ricotta cheese, but sometimes the only ricotta available
is sweet. Try it with cottage or cream cheese.

Serves 4

Preparation time:
10 minutes
Chilling time: 30 minutes

- 2 garlic cloves, chopped
- 7 oz non-sweet ricotta, cottage, or cream cheese
- 1 lb canned heart of palm, chopped, with 3 Tbsp liquid
- Salt and ground white pepper

1 Blend all the ingredients together in a blender or food processor.

2 Chill for 30 minutes before serving.

Right: Crab in its Shell

Crab in its Shell
Casquinha de Siri

This is a very popular appetizer everywhere in Brazil. It is normally served in crab shells,
which you should place on individual plates and garnish with some salad leaves to serve. If you cannot
get crab shells, use ramekin dishes in their place.

Serves 6

Preparation time: 1 hour
Cooking time: 30 minutes

- 1 lb crab meat
- Juice of 3 limes
- 4 onions
- 5 fresh tomatoes
- ½ red bell pepper
- 3 Tbsp olive oil
- 1 bay leaf
- 3 Tbsp chopped fresh parsley
- Salt and ground black pepper
- Chili powder, to taste (optional)
- 1 Tbsp flour
- 1 egg, beaten
- ⅓ cup shredded Parmesan cheese
- ¼ cup fresh bread crumbs
- Crab shells, to serve

1 Wash the crab meat, pick it clean, and remove any cartilage. Put the crab meat into a bowl and add the lime juice.

2 Put the onions, tomatoes, and bell pepper into a blender or food processor and pulse. Pour the mixture into a saucepan, add the olive oil and bay leaf. Stir well, cover, and cook for 5 minutes.

3 Preheat a 325°F oven. Add the crab meat to the saucepan. Then add the parsley, salt and pepper, and a little chili powder, if using. Cook on the stove top, covered, for 15 minutes. Then remove the lid, add the flour and egg, and stir until the sauce thickens and the egg is cooked through.

4 Remove from the heat and pour the mixture into the crab shells or ramekin dishes. Mix together the Parmesan cheese and bread crumbs, then scatter over the crab mixture.

5 Place the crab shells or ramekin dishes on a baking sheet, then cook in the oven for 10 minutes until the topping is crisp and golden brown.

Filled Bread Loaf

Pão Recheado

This is another one of my granny's secret recipes. It is ideal for picnics and parties, because it can be made in advance and you can prepare 1, 2, or 3 loaves. As an appetizer, serve two slices, garnished with salad.

1 loaf serves 4–5

Preparation time: 1 hour
Cooking time: 20 minutes
Chilling time: 1 hour

⬧ 1 square white
   sandwich loaf
⬧ 2–4 cups olive oil (for
   the various fillings and
   toppings)

*For the heart of palm
mayonnaise and carrot
mayonnaise*
⬧ 4 whole eggs
⬧ 4 egg yolks
⬧ Salt
⬧ 6 Tbsp lime juice
⬧ 1 lb canned heart of
   palm, chopped, with 5

Tbsp liquid
⬧ 2 carrots, chopped and
   cooked
⬧ 1 tsp ground black
   pepper
⬧ 2 tsp prepared mustard

For the tomato filling
⬧ 3 large onions,
   shredded
⬧ 3 garlic cloves, crushed
⬧ 6 tomatoes, blended in
   a blender
⬧ 2 Tbsp flour
⬧ 5 Tbsp shredded
   Parmesan cheese

For the spinach filling
See page 89

1 Put the loaf in the freezer for 30 minutes, so it will be easier to slice. If it crumbles a bit, don't worry because you will be covering it with mayonnaise. Using a sharp bread knife, slice the bread into ½-inch horizontal slices. Then make piles of two or three slices and remove crust.

2 For the heart of palm mayonnaise and carrot mayonnaise, put the eggs, yolks, salt, lime juice in a blender or food processor. In pulse mode, turn on and off for 5 seconds. Repeat. Turn on again and start pouring in the olive oil, little by little. The mayonnaise will start to thicken. The more oil, the richer it gets.

3 When the mayonnaise is ready, divide between two bowls. To one, add the chopped heart of palm with the reserved liquid. To the other, add the chopped cooked carrots. Add half the pepper to both bowls and mustard to the carrot mayonnaise only.

4 Heat 3 tablespoons olive oil in a saucepan, and fry onions and garlic. When translucent, add the blended tomatoes. Cook for 10 minutes.

5 Dissolve the flour in a little water and pour into the tomatoes. This sauce should be thick, but remember it thickens when it cools. Adjust seasoning.

6 Place the bottom slice of the loaf on a rectangular plate and spread the sauces over the slices, alternating them. Place the final slice on top and finally cover the whole loaf with the carrot mayonnaise.

7 Stick some toothpicks through the layers and cover with plastic wrap. Chill for 1 hour before serving.

Cheese and Bean Soup

Sopa de Feijão e Queijo

Brazilians eat beans all the time and in several different ways. This soup is a lighter version to the other in this book, because you only season with a little bacon.

Serves 6

Preparation time: 20 minutes, excluding soaking
Cooking time: 40 minutes

- ½ cup black beans
- 1 Tbsp oil
- 3½ oz slab bacon, cubed
- 2 onions, chopped
- 3 garlic cloves, chopped
- 1 bay leaf
- Salt, ground black pepper
- 1 cup of grated Gruyère or Grumentaler cheese

1 Soak the beans in advance, overnight if possible.

2 In a saucepan, heat the oil, and fry the bacon. When the bacon is nearly ready, add the chopped onions and garlic, and fry for 5 minutes more. Add the beans, the bay leaf, salt and pepper, and fresh water to cover about one third of the mixture.

3 Cook for 30 to 40 minutes, or until the beans are done, stirring occasionally. When ready, blend all the ingredients together and taste for seasoning.

4 When serving, sprinkle the grated cheese over the top.

Lebanese-style Baked Cakes

Esfihas

Apart from all the Africans, Italians, Portuguese, Spanish, Germans, Japanese, and others who emigrated to Brazil, many Arabs also live there, mainly from Syria and Lebanon. It would be wrong not to reflect this with at least one recipe in this book.

Serves 10

Preparation time:
25 minutes
Cooking time: 20 minutes

- ◇ 2 tablets of fresh bread yeast or 2 shallow Tbsp dried yeast
- ◇ 4 cups flour
- ◇ 2 eggs
- ◇ 2 Tbsp sugar
- ◇ Salt
- ◇ 1 Tbsp olive oil
- ◇ 3 Tbsp shortening

For the filling
- ◇ 1 Tbsp olive oil
- ◇ 1 large onion, grated
- ◇ 1 lb 2 oz ground beef (preferably hand-ground)
- ◇ 3 garlic cloves, crushed
- ◇ 3 large ripe tomatoes, peeled, deseeded, and chopped
- ◇ 4 Tbsp chopped fresh parsley
- ◇ Salt and ground black pepper

TIP

These little cakes make great finger food for parties.

1 Dissolve the fresh yeast in a little warm water.

2 Dust some flour over your worktop. Sift the flour, make a well in the center, and add the yeast. Knead the dough, adding the eggs, sugar, a little salt, fats, and milk. Add the milk little by little, until you form a pliable but firm dough.

3 Roll into a ball shape, then turn into a mixing bowl, cover with a dish towel, and let stand for 40 minutes to one hour, to rise.

4 Meanwhile, prepare the filling. Heat the oil in a saucepan, and fry the onion and beef for 5 minutes. It shouldn't be fully cooked, otherwise it will be too dry. Add the garlic, tomatoes, and parsley. Season with salt and pepper. Cook, uncovered, until the liquid evaporates a bit. You don't want it too dry, nor too wet.

5 Preheat a 400°F oven. Punch down the dough, then turn into balls, the size of a large lemon, and, using a rolling pin, flatten the balls into triangular shapes on a surface dusted with flour.

6 At the center of each triangle, place a level tablespoon of the filling. Picking up the three corners of the dough, close the little cake by binding them together. You should now have a little triangular parcel.

7 Place the cakes onto a flat baking sheet, which you have oiled and dusted with flour. Brush the tops with egg yolk, leave to rest for another 20 minutes, and then bake in the oven for 20 minutes, or until the dough is cooked and slightly brown.

Above: Rio de Janeiro, Brazil's stunning capital city.

Shredded Kale Soup

Caldo Verde

Another recipe inherited from the Portuguese colonizers. Delicious on a cold winter's night.

Serves 4

*Preparation time:
20 minutes
Cooking time: 30 minutes*

- ◇ 2 Tbsp olive oil
- ◇ 3 shallots, sliced fine
- ◇ 3 garlic cloves, crushed
- ◇ 3 potatoes, peeled and sliced
- ◇ 7 oz or 2 Calabresa sausages or any spicy smoked sausage, sliced
- ◇ 1 lb kale or cabbage greens
- ◇ Salt and ground black pepper

1 In a large saucepan, heat the oil and gently fry the shallots and garlic, for about 5 minutes.

2 Add the potatoes and the sausages, toss them a few times, and add water to cover half the contents. Cook over medium heat until the potatoes are soft.

3 Meanwhile, prepare the kale or greens. Wash it first, then, using a paring knife, cut the stems out and discard.

4 Make piles of five or six leaves and roll them up tightly, lengthwise, like a cigar. Then, using a very sharp knife, slice the leaves as finely as possible. Normally the shreds should not be thicker than ⅛ inch.

5 When the potatoes are done, remove from heat, and mash the mixture coarsely with a potato masher.

6 Return the saucepan to the heat, add the shredded kale or greens, and boil for 5 minutes more. Serve hot.

Langoustine Gratin in Pineapple Shell

Lagostin Gratinado em Abacaxi

Langoustines and lobster are much appreciated all over the north-eastern coast of Brazil. Very often you can order them from the little huts that serve food by the beach. The pineapple juices help to soften the meat, and if you bake the langoustines or lobster into the pineapple skin the visual effect is quite striking.

Serves 4

Preparation time:
35 minutes
Cooking time:
25–30 minutes

- 1 large or 2 small ripe pineapples
- 2¼ lb langoustines or 18 oz lobster
- Mixed herbs, to taste
- ½ cup dry white wine
- Salt and ground white pepper
- 3 Tbsp butter
- 4 shallots, finely shredded
- 4 garlic cloves, crushed
- 4 oz mushrooms
- Generous ½ cup heavy cream
- 3 Tbsp chopped fresh parsley

- 1 chayote, cubed and boiled, or 1 lb fresh peas, cooked
- 2 small carrots, cooked and cut into fine ½-inch strips
- A little shredded Parmesan cheese

1 Cut the pineapple(s) in half lengthwise, including through the crown. Using a sharp knife, make a few cuts lengthwise to make it easy to remove the flesh. Be careful not to damage the outside shell too much. Chop the flesh and reserve. Place the pineapple halves upside-down on a plate to drain off the excess juice.

2 Wash the langoustines or lobsters in fresh water. Tie some cooking string around lengthwise, to fold the tails inside before cooking.

3 Put plenty of water in a large saucepan with some salt, the mixed herbs, and the wine. Bring to a boil and throw the langoustines or lobsters into the pan. Cook for 8 to 10 minutes, or until slightly reddish-pink.

4 Drain and let cool. Cut off the string and, with a pair of kitchen scissors, make a cut into the central part of the belly. Scoop out the meat, cutting it into chunks. Remove the dark stripe that is located along the belly and discard.

5 Preheat a 375°F oven. Melt the butter in a frying pan, and fry the shallots. Add the garlic, mushrooms, and salt and pepper. Reduce the heat, add the langoustines or lobster chunks and the cream. Let cook for 5 minutes, taste for salt and pepper. Add the parsley, chayote or peas, and carrots. Remove from the heat and add the pineapple pulp.

6 Pat dry the pineapple skins with paper towels and then fill with the mixture. Scatter a little Parmesan on top and gratin in the oven for 15 minutes.

Fish and Seafood

White Fish Stew

Oyster Moqueca

Bahia-style Fish Stew

Fish Stew

Bahia-style Mussels

Flounder with Lemon Sauce

Crab Pie

Salt Cod Salad

Peppery Sauce

Oven-baked Salt Cod with Olives and Potatoes

Whole White Fish with Oyster Sauce

Cream of Cassava and Shrimps Bahia-style

Sardine Pie

Couscous São Paulo Style

White Fish Stew

—— Vatapá ——

White fish is cooked in coconut milk and flavored with fresh and dried shrimp, onion, chile, and olive oil.

Serves 8–10

Preparation time:
30 minutes
Cooking time: 40 minutes

- 2 lb fresh or frozen shrimp
- A handful of dried shrimp
- Salt and ground black pepper
- ¾ cup olive oil
- 1½ cups chopped onion
- 2 garlic cloves, chopped
- 1 red chile or 3 preserved Malagueta peppers, crushed
- 2 fresh tomatoes, peeled and chopped
- 1 sprig fresh parsley, chopped
- 1 bunch scallions, chopped fine
- 2 lb white fish, such as snapper, bass, or grouper, cut into chunks
- 1 cup canned, or ½ cup thin and ½ cup thick fresh coconut milk
- ½ cup dendê oil
- 3 slices stale white bread, crusts removed, and softened in water
- Juice of ½ lime
- 1¼ cups cassava flour (not roasted)

1 Cook the fresh and dried shrimp in a saucepan with water to cover and a pinch of salt. They will need to cook for 5–8 minutes.

2 Meanwhile, heat the olive oil in a saucepan without letting it get too hot. Throw in the onion and garlic, and stir continuously until softened but not browned.

3 Add the chiles, seasoning, tomatoes, and scallions. Add 4 cups water then add the chunks of fish. Bring to a boil and simmer for 20 minutes.

4 When the shrimp are cooked, strain, and reserve the cooking water. Add the shrimp water to the fish mixture. If you are using unshelled shrimp, add a few to the pan now and peel the rest. Then add all the shrimp to the pan.

5 Add half the coconut milk and half the dendê oil. Taste and add salt if necessary.

6 When the fish is cooked, squeeze the excess water from the bread, mash with a fork, and add to the saucepan. Pour in the lime juice.

7 Now add the cassava flour, little by little, stirring to prevent lumps forming, to thicken the sauce. Finally, add the remaining coconut milk and dendê oil. Serve with white rice and green vegetables, if you wish.

Oyster Moqueca

Moqueca de Ostra

Although this recipe calls for oyster, it can also be prepared with fish, crab, or shrimp.
Some variations have the sauce thickened with cassava flour, wrapped into banana leaves.

Serves 4

Preparation time:
20 minutes
Cooking time: 20 minutes

- 2¼ lb fresh oysters
- Juice of 2 limes
- Salt
- 2 Tbsp olive oil
- 2 large onions,

  shredded
- 2 garlic cloves, crushed
- 2 large fresh tomatoes,
  peeled and chopped
- 3 Malagueta peppers,
  chopped
- 6 Tbsp chopped fresh
  cilantro
- 1 cup thick coconut
  milk
- 2 Tbsp dendê oil

1 Clean and scrub oysters. Add oysters to boiling water and cook until they open. Drain and scoop out of shells. Pour lime juice and salt over them.

2 Heat the olive oil and fry the onions, garlic, tomatoes, peppers, and cilantro. Add oysters and three quarters of the coconut milk. Cook for 10 minutes, without the lid.

3 Add the dendê oil and the remaining coconut milk, and cook for 5 minutes more. Serve with white rice and Palm Oil Farofa (see page 83).

Bahia-style Fish Stew

Moqueca

Moquecas are generally cooked in a heavy frying pan and served in a clay dish. In Bahia, they are also
prepared with Malagueta pepper. You can either cook it very hot or serve the pepper sauce on the side.

Serves 2–4

Preparation time:
20 minutes
Cooking time: 45 minutes

- 3 lb white fish steaks,
  ideally swordfish or
  monkfish, or any firm
  white fish
- Juice of 3 limes
- 4 garlic cloves, crushed
- Salt and ground black
  pepper
- 3 Tbsp olive oil
- 3 large onions, 2
  chopped fine, 1 sliced

- 8 oz can of chopped
  tomatoes
- 4 bay leaves
- 1 yellow bell pepper, cut
  into small strips
- ½ lb peeled shrimp
  (optional)
- 1 cup thick coconut milk
- 2 Tbsp dendê oil
- ½ bunch cilantro
- ½ bunch Italian parsley
- 2 plum tomatoes, peeled
  and quartered
- 1 cup chopped, roasted
  cashews (optional)
- Hot pepper sauce or
  Malagueta pepper

1 Rinse the fish and pat it dry. Season with lime juice, half the garlic, salt and pepper. Let rest for 30 minutes.

2 Preheat 450°F oven. Heat oil in saucepan. Fry onions and rest of garlic for 5 minutes. Pour chopped tomatoes into pan, add bay leaves, salt, pepper, and yellow bell pepper. Cook for 5 minutes more. Add shrimp, if using.

3 Stirring continuously, add coconut milk, dendê oil, cilantro, and parsley. Cook for 5 minutes more.

4 Pour a half ladle of sauce into base of an ovenproof dish. Drain fish and place into dish. Pour rest of sauce over fish, add tomatoes, scatter cashews on top. Bake for 30 minutes. Serve with Palm Oil Farofa, and rice.

Right: Bahia-style Fish Stew

Fish Stew

Caldeirada de Peixe

Caldeirada de Peixe is a typical dish shared by several Brazilian states. Some ingredients vary a little according to the species of regional fish.

Serves 4–6

Preparation time:
30 minutes
Cooking time: 50 minutes

- 1 lb 2 oz tomatoes
- 1 red bell pepper
- 2 Tbsp tomato paste
- 2 onions
- 1 red chili
- Salt and ground black pepper
- 3 lb 6 oz white fish fillets such as bass or grouper
- 3 Tbsp lime juice
- ¾ cup vegetable oil
- 5 bay leaves

- 3 cups lager/pilsner beer
- 15-oz can asparagus
- 4½ oz jar of preserved mushrooms
- 1 stick butter
- 3 Tbsp flour
- 2 cups milk
- 3 Tbsp chopped fresh cilantro
- ¾ cup cassava flour (optional—see Tip)

TIP

In step 6 some of the sauce was reserved. In Brazil it is used to serve pirão with any fish stew. Simply heat the reserved sauce and add the cassava flour, little by little, to make a smooth paste—the pirão. Serve with the stew.

1 Blend tomatoes, pepper, tomato paste, half the onion, red chili, and black pepper. Reserve. Wash fish and cut into chunks. Pour over lime juice. Heat oil in a saucepan, chop rest of onion, and fry until golden.

2 Add the blended mixture to the saucepan and add the bay leaves. Put the lid on and let cook for 15 minutes. Add fish to pan, add salt. Cook for 15 minutes more.

3 Add beer, asparagus juice, and liquid from preserved mushrooms. Simmer for 20 minutes more.

4 In a small saucepan, melt the butter and dissolve the flour into it. Little by little, add the milk, and stir until it reaches a thick consistency. Reserve.

5 Add the asparagus and mushrooms to the main pan. Then add the cilantro, and taste for salt and pepper. Reserve three ladlefuls of the sauce from the fish, then stir the white sauce into the pan.

Bahia-style Mussels
Mariscos à moda Bahiana

Brazilians maintain that mussels are aphrodisiacs, so this is a popular dish. Serve it with a cold beer or cachaça—we also believe that mussels reduce the effect of alcohol!

Serves 4

Preparation time:
30 minutes
Cooking time: 20 minutes

- ◇ 36 white clams or mussels
- ◇ 3 Tbsp olive oil
- ◇ 1 bunch scallions, chopped
- ◇ 4 onions, chopped
- ◇ 5 garlic cloves, crushed
- ◇ 3 large fresh tomatoes, chopped
- ◇ 1 bunch cilantro, chopped
- ◇ Salt and ground black pepper
- ◇ 1¼ pints water
- ◇ Lime quarters, to serve

TIP

Buy any shellfish as fresh as possible and reject any that are open. After cooking, discard any that remain closed.

1 Soak the clams or mussels in fresh water while you chop the other ingredients. With a nailbrush, scrub the clams or mussels well, to remove all the sand.

2 Heat the oil in a saucepan and fry the scallions, onion, garlic, and tomatoes briefly. Carefully pour in the fresh water, bring to a boil, add the herbs, and, finally, the clams or mussels.

3 When the shellfish open up, they are ready to eat. Place them on a flat serving plate and garnish with lime quarters. Taste the sauce, and add salt and pepper as necessary, then serve in small individual bowls.

Flounder with Lime Sauce

Linguado com molho de limão

As you have probably guessed by now, we also use cassava flour for frying. The result is slightly drier than with all-purpose flour, but interesting. This recipe is for fish, but you can substitute chicken or shrimp.

Serves 4

Preparation time:
20 minutes
Frying time: 15 minutes

- ◇ 8 small flounder fillets, without the skin
- ◇ Juice of 2 limes
- ◇ Salt

TIP

Serve with Watercress and Heart of Palm Salad (see page 21) if you wish.

- ◇ 3 eggs, whisked
- ◇ 1⅔ cup cassava flour
- ◇ Oil, for shallow frying

For the sauce

- ◇ 1 small onion, grated
- ◇ 2 garlic cloves, chopped fine
- ◇ Juice of 4 limes
- ◇ 1 Tbsp chopped fresh mint
- ◇ 3 buds preserved Malagueta pepper, crushed
- ◇ Salt

1 Dip the fish in lime juice and salt. Let stand for 30 minutes. Drain, and dip each fillet into the egg mixture, and then roll in cassava flour.

2 Heat the oil and fry the fish fillets until golden, turning once.

3 For the sauce, combine all the ingredients together, mixing well. The amount of Malagueta you add will depend on the degree of spiciness you want. If the limes are too sour, add ⅓ teaspoon sugar.

Above: Sliding down dunes in Jericoacoara, Northeast Brazil.

Crab Pie

Frigideira de Siris

In Brazil, there is a huge variety of crabs: salt water, river, soft skin, white, and dark. This pie is similar to a quiche without the pastry base and can be eaten hot or cold.

Serves 4–6

Preparation time:
20 minutes
Cooking time: 40 minutes

- 2 lb fresh crab meat
- Juice of 2 limes
- 3 garlic cloves, crushed
- Salt and ground black pepper
- 1 cup fresh shredded coconut
- 2½ cups coconut milk
- 3 fresh tomatoes, quartered
- 2 onions, chopped fine
- 6 eggs
- 1 Tbsp flour
- Sliced tomatoes and onion, to garnish

1 Rinse and pick clean the crab meat. Marinate the crab in half of lime juice and garlic. Add salt, pepper, and let stand for 30 minutes to one hour.

2 Mix grated coconut with coconut milk. Reserve.

3 Preheat a 450°F oven. Using a pestle and mortar, mix the tomatoes, onion, and garlic. Add the crab meat and the remaining lime juice. Cook over low heat and add the coconut mixture. Cook, stirring, for about 15 minutes, or until thick.

4 Let cool for 10 minutes. Meanwhile, beat the egg whites until firm but not dry. Add the yolks and flour.

5 Butter an ovenproof dish and pour in half the egg mixture. Add the crab meat mixture and cover with the remaining egg mixture. Decorate with sliced tomatoes and onions.

6 Bake for 10 minutes, or until the eggs are done. Serve immediately.

Above: Largo de Pelourinho, Salvador, Northeast Brazil.

Salt Cod Salad

—— Salada Fria de Bacalhau ——

*As far back as I remember, this was always the dish served on Easter Sunday.
Brazil is a Catholic country and it was traditional not to eat meat on the Friday and Sunday
during Easter week. It is definitely another recipe inherited from the Portuguese. In Brazil
today salt cod is still imported from Portugal.*

Serves 6

Preparation time:
20 minutes
Cooking time:
20–30 minutes

- 4½ lb salt cod
  (preferable belly meat)
  soaked in advance
- 6 sweet potatoes, sliced
  into ¾-inch rounds
- 6 potatoes, sliced into
  ¾-inch rounds
- 6 small carrots
- 2 bunches of kale
- 2¼ lb West Indian
  pumpkin
- 4 tomatoes, sliced, to
  garnish

- 4 hard-cooked eggs,
  sliced, to garnish

For the dressing
- 2 cups olive oil
- ¾ cup corn oil
- ½ cup white wine
  vinegar
- 4 large onions, sliced
  fine
- 8 black peppercorns
- 4 bay leaves
- Salt, if necessary

TIP

*Although this dish may be
eaten on the day it is
prepared, the flavor improves
if it is left overnight and
eaten the next day.*

1 Cook the soaked salt cod, then let cool, reserving the cooking water. Skin the fish, then flake with your fingers, removing any bones. Cook all the vegetables in the salt cod cooking water until tender.

2 To arrange the dish, put the salt cod at the center of a large flat serving platter. Around it, distribute evenly layers of sweet potatoes, potatoes, carrots, and pumpkin, mixing the colors. Roll the kale leaves into small squares, alternating with sliced tomatoes and eggs.

3 For the dressing, heat the oils in a large saucepan. Add the onion, peppercorns, and bay leaves, frying quickly and tossing three or four times. Turn the heat off, then add the vinegar. Pour the hot dressing over the vegetables. Arrange onion slices on the cod.

4 Let cool before serving. Cover with plastic wrap and chill overnight if possible.

Peppery Sauce

Molho de Nagô

The original Molho de Nagô is made with okra and jiló (Solanum gilo). The latter is omitted in this recipe, but the result is very similar. If you like very hot food, increase the amount of Malagueta pepper. This sauce is ideal with recipes with Pirão—a cream made with stock and cassava flour (see page 34). It will make the Pirão very hot. You can also serve it separately, so people can add it to the Pirão themselves.

Preparation time: 15 minutes

- ⬧ 3 Malagueta peppers
- ⬧ 1 tsp salt
- ⬧ Juice of 1 lime
- ⬧ ⅓ cup dried shrimp, peeled and ground
- ⬧ 1 cup okra, cooked and sliced

1 Using a pestle and mortar, crush the Malagueta pepper with the salt.

2 Add the lime juice, ground dried shrimp, and okra, and crush a bit more until you reach a cream consistency.

Above: Carnival time in Olinda, Northeast Brazil.

Oven-baked Salt Cod with Olives and Potatoes

Bacalhau a Gomes de Sá

This dish is normally prepared with salt cod. If you cannot find this, use fresh cod instead, which won't need soaking. Don't forget to remove the skin.

Serves 4–6

Preparation time: 30 minutes
Cooking time: 40 minutes

- 1 lb 6 oz reconstituted salt cod
- ¼ cup olive oil
- 4 onions, sliced into fine rings
- 3 garlic cloves, chopped
- 2 tsp chopped fresh parsley

- 14 oz potatoes, boiled and cut into 1-inch slices
- Salt and ground black pepper
- 3 hard-cooked eggs, sliced
- 12 green olives, pitted and sliced

TIP

To obtain about 1 lb 6 oz of reconstituted salt cod you will need to soak about 3 lb.

1 Cook the salt cod for 5 minutes. Discard the water and skin the fish, then flake with your fingers, looking out for bones.

2 Preheat a 425°F oven. In a large saucepan, heat the olive oil and gently fry the onions, garlic, and parsley until the onions become translucent. Add the salt cod and the sliced potatoes to the saucepan and cook for 10 minutes. Taste for seasoning.

3 Transfer the mixture to a large ovenproof dish. Bake in the oven for 10 to 15 minutes. Decorate with the egg slices and green olives to serve.

Whole White Fish with Oyster Sauce

Pescada com Molho de Ostras

Pescada is the most common fish used in Brazil. It is available all over the coast, and has a silver skin, with dark silver on the back and firm white flesh.

Serves 6

Preparation time:
25 minutes
Cooking time: 30 minutes

- 1 whole white fish such as sea bream, bass, halibut, or snapper
- Salt
- 3 onions, sliced in rounds
- 1 cup white wine
- 2 Tbsp butter, softened
- ½ bunch Italian parsley, chopped

For the sauce
- 1½ lb shrimp, cleaned and peeled (reserve 6 intact, to garnish)
- 6 fresh whole oysters
- 1 jar of preserved mushrooms
- 1 Tbsp butter
- 2 Tbsp flour
- 2 egg yolks
- 2 Tbsp white wine

TIP

Oysters must be bought absolutely fresh and cooked straight away. You may want to rinse them before cooking.

1 Preheat a 375°F oven. Clean the fish, without removing the fins or head. Season with salt and place in an ovenproof dish, belly down. Around the fish, evenly distribute the onions and pour in the wine.

2 Brush with the softened butter, cover with aluminum foil, and bake in the oven. The cooking time varies according to the size of fish you have bought. It should be ready in 25 to 30 minutes. Every 5 to 8 minutes, lift the foil, and baste the fish with the sauce.

3 For the sauce, cook the shrimp and oysters in a saucepan of boiling water for about 5 minutes. Drain and reserve 2 cups of the water. Add the jar of mushrooms to the stock.

4 Melt the butter in the saucepan. Stirring, dissolve the flour into it. Little by little, pour the stock into the saucepan. Add the egg yolks to bind and the wine.

5 Pour the sauce over the fish, decorating with the oysters, parsley, and shrimp. Serve immediately.

Cream of Cassava and Shrimp Bahia-style

Bobó de Camarão

Bobó is another classic dish of Bahian and north-eastern cuisine. The result is a creamy stew of shrimp, with its consistency dictated by the purée of cassava root. It can be prepared with big shrimp but this is one dish where they can be substituted by small, frozen ones. Please note that this recipe calls for the actual cassava root and not cassava flour.

Serves 6

**Preparation time:
25 minutes**
Cooking time: 20 minutes

- 1 lb cassava/yuca, peeled and cubed
- Salt and ground black pepper
- 3 Tbsp olive oil
- 2 large onions, shredded
- 4 fresh ripe tomatoes, peeled and quartered
- 2 lb small shrimp, cleaned and peeled, tails removed
- ½ bunch cilantro, chopped fine
- 1 cup thin coconut milk
- 3 Tbsp dendê oil

1 Place the cassava or yuca in a saucepan, cover with water, add a pinch of salt, and bring to a boil. Simmer until tender enough to mash. Pour away most of the water. Mash and reserve.

2 Heat the oil and fry the onions until golden. Add the tomatoes and cook for 5 minutes. Throw in the shrimp, salt, pepper, and cilantro. Reduce the heat, cover, and cook until the shrimp are done, about 5 to 8 minutes more. Add the coconut milk and, little by little, the cassava purée, always stirring. The consistency should be the same as a thick cream. Increase the heat to medium and add the dendê oil.

3 Serve very hot with Fried Rice (see page 80), accompanied with Roasted Cassava Flour (see page 85) and Malagueta pepper sauce.

Sardine Pie

Torta de Sardinhas

This is an easy-to-make sardine pie, ideal for a quick lunchtime snack with a bowl of salad.

Serves 4–6

Preparation time:
20 minutes
Cooking time: 30 minutes

For the pastry
- ¾ cup margarine
- 2 eggs
- 1 cup Parmesan cheese
- 5 Tbsp flour
- ½ cup milk

For the filling
- 7½ oz canned sardines
- 6½ oz canned tuna
- 2 onions, sliced fine

- 4 fresh ripe tomatoes, sliced fine
- 1 cup black olives, chopped
- 1 cup green olives, chopped

For the dressing
- 9 Tbsp olive oil
- 3 Tbsp white wine vinegar
- 1 garlic clove, crushed (optional)
- Pinch of oregano
- Salt and ground black pepper

1 Preheat a 325°F oven. In a blender or food processor, mix the margarine, eggs, Parmesan cheese, flour, and milk. The pastry should be very soft. Pour the mixture into a well-buttered, large ovenproof dish.

2 Drain the sardines and the tuna well. With a fork, mash them to a paste consistency. Spread them over the pastry and evenly cover with the onions, tomatoes, and finally the olives.

3 Mix together the dressing ingredients and pour evenly over the pie. Bake in the oven for 30 minutes.

Above: Evening sun over steeple and harbor, Salvador, Bahia, Northeast Brazil.

Couscous São Paulo Style
Cuscuz à moda de São Paulo

This is a Brazilian version of couscous, an inheritance from the vast number of Arab immigrants who arrived in São Paulo State during the first half of this century. It can be eaten hot or cold as a starter or a main dish. If you cannot find flaky corn flour use coarse corn flour instead. The secret is to prepare a very fishy stock so that the flavor can mix with the flours.

Serves 6–8

Preparation time:
30 minutes
Cooking time: 15 minutes

For the pastry
- ◇ 1 lb white fish fillets, such as snapper, bass, or grouper
- ◇ Salt and ground black pepper
- ◇ 1 lb medium-size shrimp
- ◇ 1 cup vegetable oil
- ◇ 2 onions, chopped fine
- ◇ 3 garlic cloves, crushed
- ◇ 1 bunch Italian parsley, stalks only, chopped (reserve a quarter of the leaves to garnish)
- ◇ 9 oz fresh ripe tomatoes, peeled and chopped
- ◇ 1 cup peas, fresh or frozen
- ◇ ⅔ cup black olives, pitted
- ◇ 1 cup cassava flour
- ◇ 1¼ cups corn flour
- ◇ 1 bunch scallions, sliced fine
- ◇ 14½ oz canned heart of palm, drained and sliced
- ◇ 9 oz canned sardines
- ◇ ½ cup olive oil
- ◇ 3 hard-cooked eggs, sliced
- ◇ 1 green or red bell pepper, deseeded and sliced, one half sliced in rings, the other half chopped

1 Clean the fish fillets. Place in a bowl and season with salt and pepper. Then clean the shrimp. Set aside five whole shrimp, along with two sliced stalks of heart of palm, five whole black olives, a few rings of bell pepper and four whole sardines for the garnish. Chop the rest of the shrimp.

2 Heat the vegetable oil in a large saucepan. Fry the onions and garlic with a pinch of parsley. Add the white fish, shrimp, tomatoes, the chopped bell pepper, and peas. Always stirring, cook the mixture until it becomes a thick sauce and the fish has flaked. Season to taste.

3 Chop the black olives. In a mixing bowl, combine the cassava flour and corn flour, the remaining parsley stalks, the scallions, sliced heart of palm, chopped olives, and sardines.

4 Add the cassava mixture, little by little and always stirring, to the saucepan. The mixture should be damp and very compact.

5 Remove from the heat, add the olive oil, and mix well.

6 Sprinkle a deep 8-inch cake pan with water. Decorate the base of the pan with some of the reserved shrimp, heart of palm, olives, and sardines, along with some slices of hard-cooked egg. Spoon in one third of the couscous mixture and press it down firmly with your hands. Now decorate the sides of the pan with the remaining reserved fish and vegetables, and the rest of the egg slices. Carefully press in the rest of the couscous mixture, molding it firmly against the decoration with your hands. For it to remain in one piece when turned out, you must ensure the mixture is very compact.

7 Run the blade of a knife around the inside of the cake pan, place a serving plate on top, then invert the pan. The couscous will turn out onto the plate.

8 Garnish with parsley leaves before serving still warm, or chilled if you prefer.

Chicken

Chicken with Baked Egg Whites

Chicken Stew with Nuts and Dendê Oil

Baked Chicken in Bread Flour

Garlic Chicken

Chicken Stew with Rice

Chicken with Baked Egg Whites

Galinha com Mandiopã

*This is another dish that looks stunning. When it first comes out of the oven,
you can see hills of golden baked egg whites, like a soufflé.*

Serves 4

Preparation time:
15 minutes
Cooking time: 40 minutes

- 2 lb roasting chicken, quartered
- Salt and ground black pepper
- 3 Tbsp olive oil
- 4 onions, shredded
- 5 garlic cloves, crushed
- 2 x 14-oz cans plum tomatoes, chopped fine
- 3 Tbsp chopped fresh parsley
- 1 Tbsp butter
- 2 Tbsp flour
- 1 cup milk
- 4 Tbsp shredded Parmesan cheese
- 6 egg whites, beaten to a stiff peak

1 Put the chicken pieces in a large saucepan, add salt and pepper, and water to cover. Bring to a boil and cook over medium heat for 20 minutes.

2 In another saucepan, heat the oil, and fry the onions and garlic for 5 minutes. Add tomatoes, salt, pepper, and parsley. Cook uncovered for 5 minutes. In a third saucepan, melt the butter, add the flour, and stir well to dissolve. Add the milk and keep on stirring until the sauce thickens. Turn the heat off and reserve.

3 When chicken is cooked, drain. Reserve 1 cup liquid skimmed of fat. Discard rest. Leave chicken until cool then remove meat from bones.

4 Preheat a 375°F oven. Shred the chicken meat finely and add to the tomato sauce. Then add the white sauce, and check the seasoning.

5 Transfer the mixture to an ovenproof dish. Scatter the Parmesan cheese over the top. Using a wooden spoon put peaks of beaten egg whites over it. Bake for 5 to 10 minutes, or until the whites are cooked. Serve with white rice and Banana Milanese-style (see page 96).

Chicken Stew with Nuts and Dendê Oil

Xinxim de Galinha

Xinxim together with Vatapá and Acarajé are the landmarks of Bahian cuisine. Because it uses a lot of dendê oil, the sauce in this recipe is very yellowish. Xinxim is said to be Oxum, the Goddess of Camdoublé's, favorite dish and yellow her favorite color.

Serves 5

Preparation time: 2 hours
Cooking time: 50 minutes

- Juice of 3 limes
- 3 large fresh tomatoes, chopped
- 3 large onions, chopped
- 4 garlic cloves, chopped
- 2 red bell peppers, chopped
- ½ bunch of mint, chopped
- ½ bunch of cilantro, chopped
- 2 bay leaves
- 2¼ lb chicken, cut into pieces
- 5 Tbsp dendê oil
- 2 tsp grated fresh ginger root
- Salt and ground black pepper
- 1⅓ cups chopped cashews
- 1⅓ cups chopped peanuts
- 5½ oz dried ground shrimp

1 Combine the first eight ingredients in a large bowl. Add chicken pieces. Leave to marinate for 2 hours.

2 In a saucepan, heat 3 tablespoons of the oil and fry the chicken until yellow-brown. Add the marinade, ginger, salt and pepper, and some water. Cook over medium heat for around 20 minutes, keeping an eye on the water level, and adding more, if necessary.

3 When chicken is cooked, add nuts, ground shrimp, and dendê oil. Cook for 5 to 10 minutes more.

4 Serve with white rice and Roasted Cassava Flour (see page 85).

Above: Weathered waterfront dwellings, Salvador, Northeast Brazil.

Baked Chicken in Bread Flour

—— Galinha Assada com Farinha de Rosca ——

You can make this dish with bread crumbs bought in the supermarket. In Brazil, we buy bread crumbs from bakeries or make our own at home.

Serves 4

*Preparation time:
30 minutes, excluding
marinating
Cooking time: 40 minutes*

- ⋄ 3½–4 lb chicken in pieces
- ⋄ Vinha d'alhos (see page 11)
- ⋄ 5 cups fresh bread crumbs
- ⋄ 1¾ cups Parmesan cheese, shredded
- ⋄ Scant ¾ cup margarine

1 Marinate the chicken in Vinha d'alhos for one hour at least.

2 Preheat a 375°F oven. Mix the bread crumbs and Parmesan cheese.

3 Melt the margarine and dip the chicken pieces in it, coating on all sides. Roll the chicken pieces in the bread crumb mixture.

4 Put the chicken pieces into an ovenproof dish and bake for 30 to 40 minutes.

Above: Low tide in the harbor, Jericoacoara, Northeast Brazil.

Garlic Chicken

Frango a Passarinho

This chicken dish is very simple to make. The garlic is roasted and crunchy. Sometimes poussin (baby chicken) is used instead of a roasting chicken and the dish is served as an appetizer/finger food for the beach or swimming pool.

Serves 4–5

Preparation time:
45 minutes, including
marinating
Cooking time: 40 minutes

⬦ 3–3½ lb roasting chicken, cut into pieces
⬦ 1 quantity Vinha d'alhos (see page 11)
⬦ 1 Tbsp olive oil
⬦ 1 whole head of garlic, chopped
⬦ 3½ Tbsp shortening

1 Preheat a 375°F oven. Place the chicken pieces in a large bowl and cover with Vinha d'alhos. Leave to marinate for at least 30 minutes. Bake the chicken in the oven for around 20 minutes. After the first 10 minutes, turn the chicken pieces over so they bake evenly.

2 Fry the garlic in the olive oil until browned, but be careful not to burn it or it will taste bitter. Remove from the pan and set aside.

3 Take the chicken out of the oven and pour away the fat.

4 Preferably using a cast-iron pan, melt the shortening and fry the chicken pieces, turning them occasionally, until very brown and crispy.

5 When cooked, and while still very hot, toss the chicken pieces with the garlic in a bowl. Serve immediately.

Chicken Stew with Rice

Canja de Galinha

Canja is a national dish and is eaten from the north to the south, with small variations in the style of cooking.

Serves 4–6

Preparation time:
15 minutes, excluding
marinating
Cooking time:
30–35 minutes

⬦ 3½–4 lb roasting chicken, cut into pieces
⬦ 2 large onions, shredded
⬦ 4 garlic cloves, crushed

⬦ 2 fresh tomatoes, peeled and chopped
⬦ 1 red bell pepper, deseeded and chopped
⬦ 1 Tbsp white wine vinegar
⬦ Salt and ground black pepper
⬦ 6 Tbsp chopped fresh parsley
⬦ 6 Tbsp chopped fresh cilantro

1 Marinate the chicken pieces with the onions, garlic, tomatoes, red bell pepper, vinegar, and salt and pepper, for 3 hours (or a minimum of 1 hour).

2 Put the chicken pieces into a saucepan, cover with water, and cook over medium heat for 20 minutes. When you notice that the chicken starts to loosen up from the bones, add the rice.

3 Cook for 10 minutes more, or until the rice is done (it should not become soggy). Let cool, then remove any excess fat by skimming the surface. To serve, gently warm the canja through, stirring in the parsley and cilantro.

Meat

Roasted Loin of Pork

Chopped Beef Baked in a Pumpkin

Dried Meat Northeastern Style

Kidneys Southern Style

Cowboy-style Rice

Leg of Veal

Tongue with Onion Sauce

Beef Stew with Vegetables

Roasted Loin of Pork

Lombo de Porco

This is a special way of marinating the loin of pork. The meat acquires a splendid reddish color crust on the outside and a delicious flavor.

Serves 4–5

Preparation time: 15 minutes, excluding marinating
Cooking time: 1 hour 40 minutes

- 3 lb 6 oz loin of pork, preferably not very fatty
- Salt and ground black pepper
- Pinch of baking soda
- ⅓ cup flour
- 2 limes
- 2 garlic cloves, crushed
- ½ cup white wine
- A drop of olive oil

1 Rub the pork with salt. Make a few cuts over the top.

2 In a small mixing bowl, put the baking soda, flour, limes, garlic, wine, olive oil, and some pepper. Stir well and spread the mixture over the pork. Leave to rest for at least 2 hours or, ideally, overnight.

3 Preheat a 375°F oven. Place the pork in a roasting pan and cover with foil. Bake for at least 1 hour. Lift the foil frequently and baste it well. Test with a fork. When tender, remove the foil, bake for 30 to 40 minutes more, letting it become brown.

4 Allow to rest before carving. Serve with Puréed Beans Minas Gerais Style (see page 69), Fried Rice (see page 80), and Kale Minas Gerais Style (see page 82).

Above: Hilly Street, Ouro Prêto, Southeast Brazil.

Chopped Beef Baked in a Pumpkin

Picadinho na Moranga

Try to get hold of a West Indian pumpkin, otherwise use a standard variety. This dish is more commonly cooked in Brazil with shrimp or chicken, but it requires a special Brazilian cheese to get an authentic flavor. This version is with beef, which is fine without cheese.

Serves 4

Preparation time:
15 minutes
Cooking time: 1 hour

- 4–5 lb round pumpkin
- 1 lb prime cut of beef
- ¼ cup brandy
- 6 Tbsp vegetable oil or olive oil
- 4 onions, shredded
- 6 garlic cloves, crushed
- 2 green bell peppers, skinned and cubed
- Salt and ground black pepper
- 12 ripe tomatoes, peeled
- 1 red bell pepper, diced
- 6 Tbsp chopped fresh parsley
- 3 Tbsp tomato paste
- 2 Tbsp Worcestershire sauce
- 4 Malagueta peppers, with a little of the liquid (optional)
- 7 oz can corn, drained
- 2 hard-cooked eggs, chopped coarse

TIP

Instead of baking the pumpkin in step 1, if you have a large enough saucepan, you can boil it for 10 to 15 minutes.

1 Preheat a 325°F oven. Wash and dry the pumpkin. With a sharp knife, cut a lid out of the top. Using a spoon, scoop out the fiber and seeds, and discard. Rub a little oil all over the pumpkin. Put the lid back and place the pumpkin on a baking sheet. Bake for 20 to 30 minutes, but make sure you do not overcook, or it will be impossible to fill it. Liquid might accumulate inside during baking. Tip it out to prevent the base from becoming soggy, being careful not to burn yourself. When the pumpkin is cooked, remove it from the oven, but leave the oven on.

2 Grind the beef using a food processor, meat grinder, or—preferably—by hand. Put the beef into a saucepan. Pour the brandy over, and set alight. Reserve.

3 Heat the oil in a heavy frying pan. Fry the onions until translucent. Add the garlic and the chopped beef. After 5 minutes add the green peppers, then the salt and black pepper.

4 Blend the tomatoes with the red bell pepper in a blender or food processor. Pour into the frying pan, together with the parsley, tomato paste, and the Worcestershire sauce, and cook for 10 minutes more. If you like spicy food add the Malagueta peppers. It is a good idea to spice it up a little, since the pumpkin is sweet. When the meat is cooked, add the corn and the hard-cooked eggs.

5 Using a slotted spoon, to leave any excess liquid behind, fill the pumpkin with the meat mixture, and bake for 10 minutes. Serve with white rice and Roasted Cassava Flour (see page 85). When serving the beef, also scoop out a good amount of the pumpkin flesh.

Dried Meat Northeastern Style

Carne de Sol

Carne de Sol is one of the gems of Brazilian cuisine. In this book you will find some recipes with carne seca (salted, sundried meat). Carne de Sol is slightly different, because it is dried in the shade by the wind and is not so salty. You might find carne seca in some Brazilian specialty shops. If not, jerk beef is a good substitute.

Serves 4

*Preparation time:
20 minutes*

Cooking time: 20 minutes

- 2¼ lb carne de sol
- 4 Tbsp vegetable oil
- 2 large onions, cut lengthwise
- 3 garlic cloves, chopped
- 3 Tbsp chopped fresh cilantro
- 2 Tbsp snipped chives
- Salt and ground black pepper

1 Clean off the fat and cartilage, and cut the meat in large chunks. Soak the dried meat overnight, changing the water twice. Boil the meat in fresh water until soft. Shred well and reserve.

2 In a heavy saucepan, heat the oil, and fry the onions until translucent. Add the garlic, fry for 2 minutes, and finally add the shredded meat.

3 Just before serving, add the chopped herbs. Taste for salt and pepper. Serve with Purée of Pumpkin (see page 86) and white rice.

Left: The exuberance of Carnival spreads to the walls in Olinda, Northeast Brazil.

Kidneys Southern Style
Rins à moda Gaúcha

This is an extremely simple and economical dish that is quick to prepare. Originating from Rio Grande do Sul, it's a unique way of cooking kidneys, which turns them into a very tasty delicacy.

TIP

The kidneys must be trimmed before cooking. Remove any remaining suet around them, then slice them lengthwise through the middle with a sharp knife. Next, make a dip cut around the top bit where the fatty core is, and turn the kidneys inside-out, and pull the core away from the kidney. The outer membrane will come away with it. Wash before use.

Serves 4

Preparation time:
20–30 minutes
Cooking time: 5–10 minutes

⋄ **12 oz beef kidneys**
⋄ **9 oz slab bacon or smoked pancetta, cubed**
⋄ **6 Tbsp olive oil or corn oil for frying**
⋄ **Toothpicks**
⋄ **Salt and pepper to taste**

1 Having trimmed the kidneys (see tip below), cut each in half, and then in half again. Place a cube of bacon or pancetta inside each quarter and secure by pushing a toothpick right through (like a mini kabob).

2 Heat the oil in a large saucepan and fry the kidneys for 5 to 8 minutes, turning them once. When the kidneys start to release water, add salt and pepper.

3 As soon as the water dries up, turn the heat off and serve immediately. The kidneys are specially good with rice and green beans, and Roasted Cassava Flour (see page 85) is just about essential.

Cowboy-style Rice
Arroz de Carreteiro

Arroz de carreteiro is a famous dish from the south of Brazil. Carreteiros were the drivers of the ox carts, who used to cross the country taking cattle and agricultural goods. There were no storage facilities so they used to carry air-dried, salted meat, known as charque *(jerk meat). Originally, the most common jerk meat found in the south was lamb. For this recipe, you need dried meat from a Brazilian specialty shop or replace it with ground beef. My advice is to get a nice chunk of lean beef, and chop it yourself, because it tastes much better. If you cook it with fresh beef instead of dried meat, skip the steps of soaking and boiling the jerk beef.*

Serves 4–6

Preparation time: 1 hour
Cooking time: 40 minutes

- 2 lb jerk beef or ½ lb lean chopped beef
- 3 Tbsp corn oil
- 1 onion, chopped
- 2 cups white long-grain rice
- ½ a bunch Italian parsley, chopped

1 Trim the fat from the dried meat and dice it. Wash it under running water, put into a bowl, and cover with water. Soak for at least one hour.

2 Drain the meat, put into a saucepan, add 4 cups of fresh water, cover, and boil the meat for 10 minutes. Remove from the heat, drain the meat once more, and reserve 1 cup of the cooking liquid.

3 Heat the oil in a heavy saucepan and fry the onions until golden (adding the fresh meat at the same time, if using). If using the dried meat, add it when the onions are cooked, and fry for 5 to 10 minutes more, stirring all the time.

4 Wash and drain the rice. Add to the saucepan and fry for 5 minutes, always stirring so the rice does not stick to the base of the pan. Add the reserved liquid, plus 2½ cups hot water, and the parsley. (If using fresh beef, just add 3½ cups water.)

5 Let cook over high heat until the rice mixture starts to dry out. If you are not quite sure about the water amount, taste a few grains of rice. If you think they are still hard, add a little water now. If you add too much water at the beginning, you will end up serving risotto. Lower the heat, and taste for salt and pepper, being cautious with the salt if using jerk beef. When the mixture is nearly completely dry, remove from heat, cover, and let settle for 10 minutes before serving. Carreteiro is normally served on its own.

Leg of Veal
Pernil de Vitela

Brazilians eat a lot of meat. This recipe calls for veal, but leg of lamb and kid can be used instead.

Serves 4–6

Preparation time:
20 minutes
Cooking time:
1 hour 45 minutes

⬦ 5 lb 10 oz–6¾ lb leg of
   veal

For the marinade
⬦ 1 bunch fresh rosemary
⬦ 1 bunch fresh thyme
⬦ 1 bunch fresh Italian
   parsley, chopped
⬦ 1 bunch fresh chives,
   snipped
⬦ Pinch of chopped fresh
   sage
⬦ 1 cup freshly squeezed
   orange juice
⬦ 3 Tbsp olive oil
⬦ 3 Tbsp balsamic vinegar

For the stock
⬦ 4 Tbsp olive oil
⬦ 3 x 2-in pieces veal shin
⬦ 1 onion, sliced
⬦ 2 carrots, sliced
⬦ 2 celery stalks, sliced
⬦ 10–12 red peppercorns
⬦ 1 tsp salt

1 Place the leg of veal on a large dish and cover with the marinade. Seal in plastic wrap and let rest overnight.

2 The next day, fry the veal shin pieces in olive oil until brown. Add rest of stock ingredients and cook for 5 to 8 minutes. Add 12 cups water, bring to a boil. Simmer until reduced by half. Preheat a 425°F oven.

3 Place joint with marinade in a roasting pan. Cover with foil. Cook 30 minutes, remove foil, turn joint over, baste with marinade, add stock. Cook for 1 hour more.

4 Let rest before carving, and serve with white rice and a simple Roasted Cassava Flour (see page 85).

Right: Leg of Veal

Tongue with Onion Sauce
Língua em Escabeche

This is another recipe traditionally from the south of Brazil, where they say that the only things they do not eat from an animal are the bones and the feet.

Serves 4–6

Preparation time:
15 minutes
Cooking time: 40 minutes

⬦ 1 large beef tongue
⬦ Salt and 1 Tbsp ground
   pepper
⬦ 2 bay leaves
⬦ 1 cup corn oil
⬦ 4 large onions, sliced
⬦ 14 oz can puréed
   tomatoes
⬦ 1 cup red wine vinegar
⬦ 1 Tbsp flour

TIP

If you prefer, cook the tongue in a pressure cooker. Refer to the manufacturer's instructions for cooking times.

1 Place the tongue in a large saucepan, cover with water, and add seasoning and one of the bay leaves. Bring to a boil and cook until very tender, about 20–25 minutes. Skin and trim the tongue. Reserve ½ cup cooking liquid. Cut the tongue into ¼-inch slices and reserve.

3 Heat the oil in a saucepan and fry the onions until translucent. Add tongue stock, puréed tomatoes, vinegar, and salt to taste. Stir well. Cook for 5 minutes more.

4 Add the sliced tongue and cook for 5 minutes. Then dissolve the flour in ¼ cup water and pour into the pan. Stir until the sauce thickens a little. Remove from heat and serve with white rice and vegetables.

Beef Stew with Vegetables

—————————— Cozido ——————————

This is a hearty stew, great for serving on a cold winter's day. The wide variety of vegetables included means there is something for everyone's taste.

Serves 6

Preparation time: 1 hour, excluding marinating
Cooking time: 1 hour

- 2¼ lb short plate of beef
- 1 quantity *Vinha d'alhos* (see page 11)
- 1 lb 2 oz pork sausages
- 2 calabresa sausages

For the sauce
- 4 Tbsp olive oil
- 5 large onions, blended
- 5 garlic cloves, crushed
- 1 bunch chopped fresh parsley
- 1 cup homemade beef stock

- Tabasco sauce to taste
- Ground black pepper
- Scant 1¾ cups cassava flour, for the *pirão*

Vegetables
- 2 sweet potatoes
- 2 potatoes
- 2 ears of corn, cut into 1¾-in rounds
- 3 small carrots, chopped
- 1 small cabbage, chopped
- 2 chayote, chopped
- 8 oz green beans
- 8 oz pumpkin, cubed
- 1 lb kale
- 2 hard-cooked eggs, sliced, to garnish

1 Marinate the beef in the Vinha d'alhos, preferably overnight.

2 The next day, boil the sausages together. When cooked, reserve a ladleful of the cooking water and discard the rest.

3 Preheat a 250°F oven. In a very large pan, fry the onions and garlic for 5 minutes. Add the meat and cover with water. Add the parsley, then bring to a boil. Cook for 5 minutes.

4 Now add the beef stock, Tabasco, and ground black pepper. Then start adding the vegetables in the order given above. They must not be overcooked. When each type is done, place in an ovenproof dish, and keep warm in the oven. Pour a little of the sauce over the cooked vegetables, and add more water and seasoning to the saucepan if necessary. (If the meat is cooked before you have finished cooking all the vegetables, remove it to an ovenproof dish, and keep warm in the oven.)

5 When everything is cooked, place the meat, sausages, and half the sauce into one pan. You will need to bring it to a boil and then turn it off before serving.

6 In a second pan, bring the rest of the sauce to a boil, then add the cassava flour, little by little and always stirring. The *pirão* will thicken to a runny purée consistency.

7 To serve, carve half the meat, and place the whole on a large serving platter and arrange the vegetables around. Make sure they are distributed evenly to produce an attractive, colorful display. Roll the kale into little "spring roll" packages. Garnish with the egg slices. Serve the *pirão* in a separate dish, piping hot.

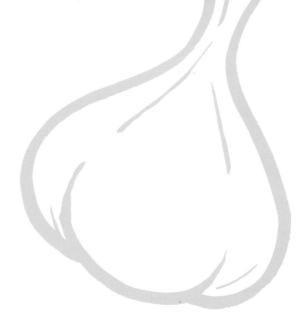

Beans

Puréed Beans Minas Gerais Style

Brazilian Black Bean and Meat Stew

Feijoada Made Simple

Vegetarian Beans

Puréed Beans Minas Gerais Style

—— Tutú de Feijao à Moda de Minas Gerais ——

Tutú was a dish prepared by slaves in eighteenth-century Minas Gerais. Today it is one of the most acclaimed dishes of Minas Gerais cuisine.

Serves 4

Preparation time:
30 minutes
Cooking time: 1½ hours

- 2 cups Fradinho/pinto/ cranberry beans, soaked overnight
- 5½ oz slab bacon, chopped fine
- 1 bay leaf
- A handful of parsley, stalks and leaves
- separated
- ½ cup cassava flour
- 1 large red onion, chopped
- 3 garlic cloves, crushed
- 8 oz fresh tomatoes, peeled, deseeded, and chopped rough
- 3 Malagueta peppers, crushed
- Salt
- 2 hard-cooked eggs, sliced

1 Drain and rinse the beans. Place in a large saucepan with the bacon, bay leaf, and parsley stalks. Cover with water and cook for about 30 minutes.

2 Remove from the heat, discard the herbs, strain, and reserve the cooking liquid. Purée the beans and bacon in a blender or food processor. Put the purée back into the saucepan and, little by little and always stirring, add the cassava flour.

3 In a second saucepan, put 2 cups of the reserved cooking liquid with the onion, garlic, tomatoes, and Malagueta peppers. Bring to a boil and cook until the vegetables are tender and the sauce has reduced. Add salt, to taste, and the parsley leaves. Then purée the sauce in a blender or food processor.

4 Mix sauce into the bean purée, heat through. Serve on a flat plate. Garnish with eggs and Kale Minas Gerais Style (see page 82). Serve with white rice and Roasted Loin of Pork (see page 56).

Brazilian Black Bean and Meat Stew

— Feijoida Completa a Moda Brasileira —

There is a saying in Brazil that whenever you prepare feijoada you can feed as many people as turn up for lunch. If fifteen people arrive when you were expecting ten, add a little more water to the sauce, thicken again, and serve with the confidence that no one will go hungry. This traditional dish is best cooked a day or two in advance. Let cool and then chill until required.

Serves 8–10

Preparation time: 3 hours, one day ahead
Cooking time: 4 hours minimum

- Generous 3 cups black beans
- 3 Tbsp corn oil or sunflower oil
- 3 large onions, chopped
- 5 large garlic cloves, chopped
- 4 bay leaves
- ½ tsp salt
- 1 tsp ground black pepper
- 4 Tbsp chopped fresh parsley
- 2 Malagueta peppers

Meat
- 8 oz air-dried and salted meat (*carne seca*)

TIP

Instead of raising the heat to thicken the sauce, as described in step 6, some people prefer to add a tablespoon of flour or cornstarch, mixed to a runny paste with water. Others simply mash some of the beans when fully cooked and return them to the pan. These two methods should be done when reheating the stew before serving.

- 8 oz smoked pork ribs
- 8 oz each dried salted pig's ears, tails, and trotters
- 1 fresh beef tongue
- 1 lb pork sausages
- 8 oz *paio* (Brazilian/Portuguese sausages) or blood sausage
- 8 oz calabresa or chorizo sausages
- 8 oz salted slab bacon, diced

1 The evening before cooking, soak the dried meat (*carne seca*) and pork ribs together. In a separate container, soak the pig's ears, tails, and trotters. Change the water in both containers at least once. Soak the black beans overnight too.

2 The next day, rinse the soaked meats, place in a large saucepan, cover with water, and bring to a boil. Reduce the heat and simmer for 5 minutes. Drain and discard the water. Repeat. This gets rid of the excess fat and salt. Trim the pig's ears and the tongue. Set the meats aside. In a separate pan, cook the ox tongue with a pinch of

salt, pepper, and one of the bay leaves until very tender. Skin and trim the tongue. Reserve.

3 Slice the pork sausages, *paio*, and calabresa or chorizo sausages. Heat 1 tablespoon of the oil in a frying pan and fry the sausages until slightly brown on both sides. Set aside, reserving the oil.

4 Drain and rinse the beans, then set aside. Heat the remaining oil in a very large, high-sided saucepan, then fry the onion and diced bacon. When the onions become translucent, add the garlic. Cook until the garlic browns slightly, then add the beans. Fry for 1 to 2 minutes, stirring.

5 Then add enough cold water to cover the beans by half their depth again, the bay leaves, salt, and pepper. Add very little salt—remember that some of the meats are salted—and adjust at the end of the recipe.

6 Now add the reserved meats, the sausages with their oil, and water to cover the beans by one quarter of their depth again. Let simmer for an hour, stirring continuously. During this time, bring to a boil two or three times. This will help thicken the sauce (and should be repeated five times more during the last hour of cooking—but see Tip).

7 After this, add the parsley and simmer for 15 minutes more, or until all the beans are cooked right through.

8 To serve, first reheat the stew and check the seasoning. Decant a few ladlefuls of the sauce into a separate saucepan and add the Malagueta peppers and a little of the reserved liquid. Heat through and serve separately to allow people to help themselves. The other traditional accompaniments are white rice, Roasted Cassava Flour (see page 85), Kale Minas Gerais Style (see page 82), and sliced oranges. Either serve the stew from the pot or set the meats out on one large or several small serving platters, with the beans in a separate dish. Traditionally the tongue is sliced and placed centrally, the pig's ears, tails, and trotters are set on one side, and the rest of the meats are set on the other. Because this dish is so filling, Brazilians eat it for lunch, not supper, usually on Wednesdays or Saturdays.

Feijoada Made Simple

Feijoada Simples

*This is a simpler version of Feijoada. It does not have pig trotters, ears, and tails.
In any case, it still tastes very, very delicious.*

Serves 4–6

*Preparation time: 3 hours,
one day ahead*
*Cooking time: 3 hours
minimum*

- Scant 1½ cups black
  beans
- 3 Tbsp corn oil
- 2 large onions,
  chopped
- 4 large garlic cloves,
  chopped
- 2 bay leaves
- Salt and ground black
  pepper

- 2 Tbsp chopped fresh
  parsley
- 1 Malagueta pepper,
  chopped
- 1 Tbsp cornstarch

Meat
- 8 oz smoked pork ribs
- 8 oz smoked loin pork
- 8 oz pork sausages
- 8 oz *paio* (Brazilian
  sausages)
- 8 oz calabresa or
  chorizo sausages
- 8 oz salted slab bacon,
  diced fine

1 The evening before cooking, soak the smoked meats together in a bowl. Soak the black beans overnight too.

2 The next day, rinse the soaked meats, place in a large saucepan, cover with water, and bring to a boil. Reduce heat and simmer for 5 minutes. Drain and discard water. Repeat. This will get rid of excess fat and salt.

3 Slice the sausages. Heat 1 tablespoon of the oil in a frying pan. Fry the sausages until slightly brown on both sides. Set aside, reserving the oil.

4 Drain and rinse the beans. In a large, high-sided saucepan, heat the remaining oil, then fry the onions and diced bacon. When the onions are translucent, add the garlic. When the garlic is slightly browned, add the beans. Fry for 1 or 2 minutes, stirring.

5 Then add enough cold water to cover the beans by half their depth again, the bay leaves, and salt and pepper, being cautious with the salt (see Brazilian Black Bean and Meat Stew). Bring to a boil, then simmer for 30 to 40 minutes. The beans should then be softened but not cooked right through.

6 Now add the meats, the reserved sausages and their oil, and water to cover the beans by one quarter of their depth again. Let simmer for an hour. After this, add the parsley and simmer for 15 minutes more.

7 To serve, reheat the stew and check the seasoning. Decant a few ladlefuls of the sauce into a separate saucepan and add the Malagueta pepper. Heat through and serve separately. Dissolve the cornstarch in a little water, then add to the stew, always stirring, to thicken the sauce. Arrange the meats on a serving platter and the beans in a separate dish. Serve with white rice and Roasted Cassava Flour (see page 85), with a green vegetable and orange slices.

Vegetarian Beans
Feijão Vegetariano

Here is a meatless version of Feijoada for vegetarians. The inclusion of sweet potatoes and eggplant provides variety in both texture and taste.

Serves 4

Preparation time:
15 minutes
Cooking time: 1 hour

- 3 Tbsp corn oil or sunflower oil
- 2 large onions, chopped
- 4 large garlic cloves, chopped
- ¾ cup black beans, soaked overnight
- Salt and ground black pepper
- 3 carrots, sliced
- 2 sweet potatoes
- 1 eggplant, cubed
- 2 bay leaves
- 4 Tbsp parsley
- ⅓ cup red wine

1 Heat the oil and fry the onions and garlic until slightly browned.

2 Drain the beans and fry them with the onions and garlic for 5 minutes. Cover with water, add salt and pepper, and cook for 20 minutes.

3 Add the vegetables and herbs, the wine, and taste for salt and pepper. Cook for 25 minutes more, or until all the ingredients are tender.

Above: Brazilian joie de vivre, Salvador, Northeast Brazil.

Barbecues
and Sauces

Vinegar-based Sauce

Southern Seasoning

Leftover Beans with Cassava Flour

Onion Salad

Eggplant Salad with Apples

Vinegar-based Sauce
Molho Vinagrete

In São Paulo, this sauce is used to marinate the meats and also as an accompaniment, after the meat is ready. Brazilians from the south think it is silly to marinate meats in vinegar. My advice is that you follow the recipe for Southern Seasoning (see page 76) and use this sauce as an accompaniment.

Makes 1½ cups

Preparation time: 10 minutes

- 2 onions, chopped fine
- 3 garlic cloves, chopped very fine
- 3 fresh tomatoes, peeled, deseeded, and chopped very fine
- ¼ tsp sugar
- 6 Tbsp chopped fresh parsley
- 4 Tbsp chopped fresh cilantro
- 1 cup white wine vinegar
- Salt and ground black pepper

1 Combine all the ingredients well in a bowl.

2 Add salt and pepper to taste.

3 Serve in a small bowl, so people help themselves.

Left: The sun setting over Salvador, Northeast Brazil.

Southern Seasoning
Salmora

This is one of the secret methods of south Brazilian barbecues. It creates a perfectly seasoned, succulent joint of barbecued meat which can be served with various salads.

⋄ **Water**
⋄ **Cubed salt**
⋄ **A small bunch of Italian parsley, tied with string**

Barbecues in the south of Brazil are large, brick-built affairs which are lit several hours in advance and involve the very slow cooking of huge pieces of meat, on a long metal skewer.

1 Before the meat is cooked, hold it on its skewer over a long oblong wooden bowl, which contains a solution of water and thick salt. Dip the bunch of parsley into the salty water and brush the meat all over. Some pieces of salt not dissolved by the water may remain on the meat and get stuck to the flesh, especially to the fatty bits.

2 Then place the skewer over the fire. Halfway through the cooking time, repeat the same salting operation.

3 When meat is ready to eat (but still pink on inside) remove it from barbecue. Rest the end of the skewer against a hard surface; the ends of the skewer should be hit with a wooden stick to remove excess salt.

4 The meat is now properly seasoned and ready to be sliced.

Leftover Beans with Cassava Flour

Feijão Mexido

This is a great way of using up leftover beans. Serve it as an accompaniment to barbecues. The number it serves depends on the quantity of leftovers you have.

*Preparation time:
10 minutes*

Cooking time: 15 minutes

- **Leftover cooked black beans or Brazilian Black Bean and Meat Stew (see page 70)**
- **1 red chili, chopped fine**
- **Chopped fresh parsley**
- **1 cup cassava flour**

1 Warm the beans or Feijoada gently in a saucepan. If your mixture has little sauce, add some water. Stir in the chili and parsley.

2 Add the cassava flour, little by little and always stirring, until the mixture is thick and smooth.

3 Serve hot or at room temperature.

Onion Salad
Salada de Cebolas

This is a typical accompaniment for southern barbecues. If you soak the onions, you get rid of the acidity and bitterness.

Serves 6

Preparation time:
45 minutes

- 5 onions, cut into rounds
- 1 Tbsp sugar
- Salad dressing of choice

1 Soak the onions in warm water mixed with sugar for 30 minutes.

2 Drain well, then toss in salad dressing.

Eggplant Salad with Apples
Salada de Berinjela com Maçã

This salad is baked and then cooled before serving. It makes a good accompaniment to barbecued meats.

Serves 4

Preparation time:
15 minutes
Cooking time:
30–35 minutes

- 4 eggplants, cubed
- 3 apples, cubed
- 2 red bell peppers, diced
- 2 green bell peppers, diced
- Scant 1½ cups golden raisins
- Scant 1½ cups raisins
- 1 cup white wine vinegar
- 1 cup olive oil
- Pinch of salt

1 Preheat a 325°F oven. Mix all the ingredients together in an ovenproof dish.

2 Bake for 30 to 35 minutes, then remove from the heat. Let cool, and serve as a salad.

Accompaniments

Fried Rice

Fried Coconut Rice

Kale Minas Gerais Style

Bahian-style Corn

Roasted Cassava Flour

Palm Oil Farofa

Purée of Pumpkin

Dried Shrimp with Greens

Spinach Cream

Corn Cream

Prune Cream

Chayote Soufflé

Bahia-style Okra

Straw Potatoes

Milanese-style Banana

Fried Rice

Arroz

You might serve this rice with the onion and garlic over it or you may remove these and serve only the rice like Brazilians do. In any case the flavor is good.

Serves 4

Preparation time:
10 minutes
Cooking time: 20 minutes

- 2 cups rice
- About 3 Tbsp sunflower or corn oil
- 1 small shallot, sliced fine
- 1 garlic clove, crushed
- Salt

1 Wash the rice and drain. Pour enough oil into a saucepan to cover the base, about 3 tablespoons. Heat the oil and throw in the shallot and garlic. When they are becoming golden, throw in the drained rice. Stir with a wooden spoon, frying rice in the mixture.

3 Measure twice as much hot water as rice, and add to the pan. Add a pinch of salt. Bring the rice to a boil, lower the heat, and partially cover the saucepan.

4 When the water has evaporated to below the level of rice in the saucepan, remove the lid. With a chopstick make four or five holes in the rice to allow the water to evaporate completely. At this stage you should keep an eye on it to ensure it does not burn.

5 When the rice is nearly fully dry, remove from the heat. Ideally you should then let it settle for 20 minutes. Just before serving, fluff up the rice with a fork.

Fried Coconut Rice

Arroz com Coco

The addition of coconut milk to the water gives the rice a wonderful aroma and taste.

Serves 4

Preparation time:
10 minutes
Cooking time: 20 minutes

- 2 cups rice

- About 3 Tbsp sunflower or corn oil
- 1 small shallot, sliced fine
- 1 garlic clove, crushed
- 1 cup thick coconut milk
- Salt

1 Measure out the required amount of rice, wash it, and drain well in a strainer.

2 Pour enough oil into a saucepan to cover the base, about 3 tablespoons. Heat the oil and throw in the shallot and garlic. When they are becoming slightly golden, throw in the drained rice. Stir with a wooden spoon, frying rice in the mixture.

3 Carefully pour in the coconut milk, then make up the liquid measure to twice that of rice with water. Add a pinch of salt. Bring the rice to a boil, lower the heat, and partially cover the saucepan.

4 When the liquid has evaporated to below the level of rice in the saucepan, remove the lid. With a chopstick make four or five holes in the rice to allow the liquid to evaporate completely. At this stage you should keep an eye on it to ensure it does not burn.

5 When the rice is nearly fully dry, remove from the heat. Ideally you should then let it settle for 20 minutes. Just before serving, fluff up the rice with a fork.

Right: Fried Coconut Rice

Kale Minas Gerais Style
Couve à Moda de Minas Gerais

This fried kale makes an ideal accompaniment for Brazilian Black Bean and Meat Stew (see page 70) and Puréed Beans Minas Gerais Style (see page 69). It is also good served with chicken and roasted pork.

Serves 6

Preparation time: 10 minutes

Frying time: 5 minutes

- 1½ lb kale
- 3 Tbsp olive oil
- 2 shallots, chopped very fine
- 2 garlic cloves, crushed
- Salt and ground black pepper

1 Wash the kale. Cut out the tough stems and discard.

2 Taking five or six leaves at a time, roll them up tightly like a cigar. Fold them in half, and again in half. Now tuck the edges in. Then, using a very sharp knife, slice the kale as finely as possible. The shreds should not be thicker than ⅛ inch, and finer if possible.

3 Heat the oil to medium heat, and fry the shallots and garlic. Add the kale and stir-fry for 5 minutes, until the shreds start softening, but are still crisp. Serve hot.

Palm Oil Farofa

Farofa de Dendê

Farofa de Dendê is more commonly eaten in the northeast to accompany dishes with shrimps and stews.

Serves 5

Preparation time: 10 minutes
Cooking time: 10 minutes

◇ **4 Tbsp dendê oil**
◇ **2 onions, shredded**
◇ **5½ cups cassava flour**
◇ **5½ oz dried shrimp, ground**
◇ **Salt and ground black pepper**

1 In a saucepan, heat the oil, and fry the onions until slightly brown.

2 Mix the cassava flour and dried shrimp together, then add to the saucepan. Stir very quickly from the center of the pan outward.

3 Add salt and pepper to taste, and serve hot.

Left: Cascade of rooftops, Salvador, Northeast Brazil.

Bahian-style Corn
Acaçá

Acaçá is another very typical Bahian delicacy. In Bahia, they normally soak the corn for two nights until it goes sour. Then they cook it and wrap in banana leaves. It is a great accompaniment for stews and dishes cooked with olive oil or palm oil.

Serves 4

Preparation time: 10 minutes, excluding soaking
Cooking time: 10 minutes

⋄ **2 cups of corn on the cob**
⋄ **Salt**
⋄ **8 banana leaves (optional)**

1 Take the corn out of the cobs. Cover and soak in cold water to soften.

2 As soon as the corn is swollen, pass it through a meat grinder or blend it in a blender or food processor with a bit of water.

3 Add some salt and pour the mixture into a saucepan, add ⅓ pint water, and cook over low heat until creamy.

4 If you are going to wrap the acaçá in banana leaves, steam them first to soften.

5 Serve cold.

Roasted Cassava Flour
Farofa

This is a basic recipe for farofa, which is a good accompaniment to any stew, meat, fish, or beans. When preparing farofa for beans, use bacon. When preparing farofa for chicken, traditionally, giblets are used. For fish, use small shrimp.

Serves 6

Preparation time:
20 minutes
Cooking time: 10 minutes

◇ **9 cups unroasted cassava flour**
◇ **5½ oz slab bacon, chopped**
◇ **2 sticks butter, cubed**
◇ **2 bananas, sliced (optional)**
◇ **3½ oz golden raisins**
◇ **3 hard-cooked eggs, chopped**
◇ **Salt**

1 In a large frying pan, roast the cassava flour over very low heat. Using a wooden spatula, keep stirring very quickly. Do not allow to burn. When it changes color to light amber, remove from heat. Pour into a bowl.

2 Now fry the bacon over low heat until tender. Add the butter and let it melt. When the butter is melted, add the cassava flour. Keep stirring until the cassava flour has absorbed all the butter. The consistency should be like a crumble topping.

3 Gently stir in the sliced bananas, golden raisins, and chopped egg. Add salt and pepper to taste.

Purée of Pumpkin
Quibebe

Quibebe is a name of African origins, from Angola. Pumpkin is one of the most used ingredients in northeastern cuisine. This makes an ideal accompaniment to Dried Meat Northeastern Style (see page 60).

Serves 4

*Preparation time:
15 minutes*

Cooking time: 20 minutes

⬦ **1 lb 2 oz ripe pumpkin, preferably West Indian**
⬦ **Salt and ground black pepper**
⬦ **3 Tbsp vegetable oil**
⬦ **2 onions, chopped fine**
⬦ **2 garlic cloves, crushed**
⬦ **4 Tbsp chopped fresh Italian parsley**

1 Peel the pumpkin and cut into 1-inch cubes. Cover with water, add a good amount of salt, and cook until quite tender.

2 Heat the oil in a saucepan and fry the onions and garlic. Add the pumpkin, and salt and pepper.

3 Mash the pumpkin with a potato masher, scatter the parsley over, and serve hot.

Above: A mosaic of roof tiles in Ouro Prêto, Southeast Brazil.

Dried Shrimp with Greens
Efó

This is another famous Bahian dish, of African origin. Serve with Bahian-style Corn (see page 84), or any other Bahia dish.

Serves 4

Preparation time: 20 minutes
Cooking time: 20 minutes

- 1 lb shrimp, cooked and peeled
- 3 Tbsp dried shrimp
- 2 garlic cloves
- 3 onions, quartered
- 4 Malagueta peppers
- 1 Tbsp chopped fresh cilantro
- 2½ lb spinach, mustard greens, cabbage greens, chopped rough
- 2 Tbsp olive oil
- 2 large tomatoes, peeled, deseeded, and quartered
- Salt and ground black pepper
- ¼ cup cashews
- ¼ cup peanuts
- 1 cup each thin and thick coconut milk or 2 cups canned coconut milk
- 2 Tbsp dendê oil

1 Blend the fresh and dried shrimp with the garlic, onions, Malagueta peppers, and cilantro.

2 Put the spinach or other greens into a saucepan with a little water, cover, and steam for 5 minutes.

3 Meanwhile, heat the olive oil in a small frying pan and fry the shrimp mixture until slightly brown. Then add to the saucepan, together with the tomatoes, and salt and pepper. Keep an eye on it so it does not burn.

4 Blend the cashews and peanuts with the coconut milk, and add to the pan. Add the dendê oil and cook over very low heat for another 10 minutes, stirring.

Left: Colorful carnival, Olinda, Northeast Brazil.

Spinach Cream
Creme de Espinafre

This creamed spinach dish makes a colorful accompaniment to any main course dish—meat, poultry, fish, or beans.

Serves 4

Preparation time: 10 minutes
Cooking time: 15 minutes

- ⋄ 3 Tbsp oil
- ⋄ 1 large onion, chopped fine
- ⋄ 1 lb spinach, chopped fine
- ⋄ 1 cup milk
- ⋄ Salt and ground black pepper
- ⋄ 1 Tbsp flour

1 Heat the oil in a large pan and fry the onion until it is golden.

2 Throw the spinach into the pan, pour in ½ cup of the milk, and cook for 5 minutes. Add salt and pepper.

3 Dissolve the flour in the remaining milk and then add to the pan. Stir continuously until a cream consistency is reached.

Corn Cream

Creme de Milho

This recipe is an ideal accompaniment to meat and fish dishes.

Serves 6

*Preparation time:
10 minutes*
Cooking time: 15 minutes

- 1 beef stock cube
- 11 oz canned corn, with its liquid
- Generous 2 cups milk
- Salt and ground black pepper
- 3 Tbsp cornstarch
- Chopped fresh parsley, to garnish
- Water

1 Measure out just over 2 cups water and reserve about ½ cup in a small bowl. Place the rest in a saucepan and bring to a boil. Dissolve the stock cube in it and then add the canned corn and its liquid. Lower the heat and stir in the milk. Taste and season. Do not boil.

2 Now dissolve the cornstarch in the reserved water. Add to the saucepan, always stirring. The sauce will now start to thicken. When you reach a consistency of cream, turn the heat off.

3 Serve warm and sprinkle the chopped parsley on top to garnish.

Above: The splendor of the Iguassu Falls, on the Brazil/Argentina border.

Prune Cream
Creme de Ameixas

This is a delicious accompaniment for Roasted Loin of Pork (see page 56).

Serves 4–6

Preparation time:
10 minutes
Cooking time: 30 minutes

- ◇ **2¼ cups prunes (pitted or not)**
- ◇ **8 Tbsp granulated or granulated brown sugar**

1 Put the prunes into a medium-size saucepan, add 1⅔ cups cold water, and half the sugar. Bring to a boil, cook

> **TIP**
>
> *If you have a bit left over after a meal, this is also an ideal accompaniment for granola or yogurt in the morning, or as a sauce for vanilla ice cream.*

for about 5 minutes, and then reduce the heat. Cover and simmer for about 25 minutes.

2 With a fork, mash the prunes a bit. If the prunes were unpitted, now is the time to get rid of the stones.

3 Now add the rest of the sugar to the sauce and return to the heat. At this stage, you should check the level of water and add more if necessary. You want to achieve a cream consistency. For this, you should have enough water to bring the prunes back to a boil once more. Cook for 10 minutes, raising and lowering the heat at least four times to help thicken the sauce. Serve warm or at room temperature.

Above: Long evening shadows in Olinda, Northeast Brazil.

Chayote Soufflé
Suflê de Chuchú

Chayote is a very typical Brazilian vegetable. It resembles a pear in shape and it is light green. Do not buy too hard or too soft, but firm. It is easy to find in Latin American and Caribbean shops.

Serves 4

Preparation time:
20 minutes
Cooking time:
20–25 minutes

- 2 Tbsp butter
- 1 large onion, shredded
- 2 Tbsp flour
- ¾ cup hot milk

- 6 Tbsp shredded Parmesan cheese
- 2 egg yolks, whisked
- 9 oz chayote, peeled, cooked, and chopped
- Salt and ground black pepper
- 2 egg whites, beaten to a stiff peak
- 1 tsp baking powder

1 Preheat a 375°F oven. In a saucepan, melt butter and fry onions until translucent. Add flour and dissolve it into butter. Add the milk and stir until mixture thickens.

2 Remove the pan from the heat. Add the Parmesan cheese, reserving 1 tablespoon, the egg yolks, and the chayote. Mix well and season to taste.

3 Fold in the egg whites and the baking powder. Pour the mixture into a well-buttered ovenproof dish and scatter the reserved Parmesan on top. Bake for 12 to 15 minutes, or until the top is brown. Serve very hot.

Bahia-style Okra
Carurú

*This is another Afro-Brazilian recipe. The ancient technique called for all the ingredients to be ground on a **pedra-de-ralar**, a grinding-stone.*

Serves 6

Preparation time:
15 minutes
Cooking time: 25 minutes

- Juice of 3 limes
- Salt and ground black pepper
- 2 lb of firm, green okra, trimmed and cut into small pieces
- 5 Tbsp dendê oil
- 2 onions, ground
- 3 garlic cloves, crushed
- 3 sprigs of cilantro, chopped

- ½ cup peanuts, chopped rough
- ½ cup cashews, chopped rough
- 4 Tbsp dried shrimp, ground
- A few drops preserved Malagueta pepper liquid (optional)

TIP

If you have never prepared okra before, you will notice a slightly sticky liquid oozes out when cut. If you wash them and pat dry well you will reduce the amount of liquid.

1 In a large bowl, add a pinch of salt to the lime juice and allow the salt to dissolve. Then toss the okra in the lime juice.

2 Now heat the dendê oil in a heavy frying pan, fry the onions and garlic until golden, then add the cilantro, and fry for a minute more.

3 Add okra to the pan, plus peanuts, cashews, and salt and pepper. Scatter over the shrimp. Add 1 cup water. Place lid on pan, and let simmer for 20 minutes.

4 If you like hot food, add some drops of the liquid from preserved Malagueta peppers. Serve the carurú hot, with rice and as an accompaniment to any Bahian dish.

Right: Bahia-style Okra

Straw Potatoes
Batata Palha

This is an easy way to prepare fried potatoes. Brazilians eat them with saucy dishes and stews.

Serves 4

Preparation time:
20 minutes
Frying time: 20 minutes

- 4 potatoes
- Salt
- Oil, for frying

TIP

The great thing about these potatoes is that you can store them in an airtight jar and eat them later. They will lose a bit of crunchiness, but not a lot.

1 Peel and cut the potatoes in half. Using the shredder disk of your food processor, shred them finely. (Alternatively, shred them with a hand-held shredder.)

2 Place the potato on a dry dish towel and pat dry. Then sprinkle with salt.

3 Heat the oil to very hot. Fry the potatoes, little by little or they will get stuck together. Drain on paper towels to dry before serving.

Milanese-style Banana
Banana à Milanesa

In Brazil, everything that is dipped in egg and bread crumbs is called "Milanese style." This fried banana dish partners black beans and it is also delicious with chicken. It is very easy to make.

Serves 6

Preparation time:
20 minutes

Frying time: 15 minutes

- ◇ **4 eggs, beaten**
- ◇ **1½ cups fresh bread crumbs**
- ◇ **6 semi-ripe bananas**
- ◇ **Oil for shallow frying**

1 Place the eggs in a shallow dish. Place the bread crumbs in a second dish.

2 Dip the bananas, one by one, first into the egg and then straight away into the bread crumbs. Make sure they are evenly coated.

3 Heat the oil in a heavy frying pan. Fry the bananas, one by one, turning them over when slightly brown. As they are cooked, remove with a slotted spoon onto paper towels. Serve warm.

Desserts and Puddings

Tropical Fruit Salad

Orange Pudding

Banana Marrons

Coconut Manjar

Coconut Pudding

Burnt Coconut Sweets

Avocado Cream

Coconut Sweets

Pumpkin with Shredded Fresh Coconut

Coconut Custard

Three-layered Pudding

Coffee Ice Cream

Passionfruit Tart

Cream of Eggs and Milk

Layered Cookie Tart

Cream of Egg Yolks with Brandy

Meringue Soufflé

Chocolate and Coconut Kisses

Little Coconut Kisses

Passionfruit Manjar

Chocolate and Coconut Cake

Coffee Cake

Mango Mousse

Cassava Cake

Corn Cake

Tropical Fruit Salad

Salada de Frutas Tropical

There are endless varieties of tropical fruits in Brazil. This is because, for example, some fruits from the northeast cannot be found in the southern states. For this salad I have chosen fruits typically found easily outside Brazil.

Serves 4

Preparation time:
20 minutes

- Juice of 3 oranges
- 5 passionfruit
- 1 papaya
- 1 mango
- 1 small pineapple
- 1 small melon
- 2 apples
- 2 star fruit
- 1 banana
- Ice cubes

1 Blend the orange juice with the passionfruit pulp. Strain and discard the seeds.

2 Cut the papaya, mango, pineapple, melon, and apples into small cubes and slice the star fruit.

3 Put the prepared fruit into a bowl and add the juice.

4 When you are ready to serve, slice the banana and add to the bowl, along with some ice cubes. Stir and serve.

Orange Pudding

Pudim de Laranja da Maria Ondina

This recipe is already published in two cookbooks. Maria Ondina has been one of my mother's best friends since childhood.

Serves 6

Preparation time: 20 minutes

Cooking time: 30–35 minutes

- ◇ **12 egg yolks**
- ◇ **9 egg whites**
- ◇ **2½ cups sugar**
- ◇ **Scant ¾ cup freshly squeezed orange juice**

1 Beat all the ingredients together well. Pour into a cake tin caramelized with sugar (3 Tbsp sugar melted in 2 tsp water, brushed onto the tin). Preheat the oven to 350°F. Put the cake tin in a roasting tin half filled with hot water. Transfer to the oven and cook for 30–35 minutes until risen and springy to the touch.

2 Remove from the heat. Let cool for 15 minutes, then chill for 1 hour. Remove from the refrigerator and turn the pudding out onto a serving plate.

Banana Marrons

Bananinha

Bananinhas are one of the best reminders of a Brazilian childhood. It is a recipe that certainly reminds me of my granny and how she used to treat her grandchildren.

Makes 8–12

Preparation time: 5 minutes

Cooking time: 25 minutes

- ◇ **8 small bananas**
- ◇ **Generous ⅔ cup sugar**
- ◇ **¾ cup red wine**
- ◇ **1 tsp of vanilla extract**
- ◇ **Sugar, for rolling.**

1 Using a fork, mash the bananas well into a pulp. Put the bananas into a small saucepan and add the sugar. Cook over low heat, stirring until the pulp reduces and you are able to see the base of the pan.

2 Add the red wine and repeat the process until you can see the base of the pan. Add the vanilla and transfer mixture to a flat, well-buttered surface.

3 Leave for 6 to 8 hours. Then cut into small banana shapes, roll in sugar, then let them dry well. Wrap in candypaper and store in an airtight container.

Coconut Manjar
Manjar de Coco

The traditional recipe for manjar is with milk, coconut, and corn flour cooked in a Bain-marie on the stove. Here is a simplified version, commonly used in Brazil. The word Manjar is a corruption from the French manger and Italian mangiare, meaning "to eat." In Portuguese it also means delicate and delicious food that feeds the spirit and soul.

Serves 4–6

Preparation time: 20 minutes
Cooking time: 20 minutes

⋄ 1 sachet gelatine
⋄ 6 egg whites
⋄ 1 14 fl oz can sweetened condensed milk
⋄ 1 cup heavy cream
⋄ 1 14 fl oz can of coconut milk
⋄ ½ cup shredded coconut, preferably fresh

For the sauce
⋄ ¾ cup prunes, pitted
⋄ 5 Tbsp superfine sugar

TIP

If you would prefer a thicker sauce, add more sugar once the prunes are soft, bring to a boil again, and then set aside.

1 Pour the gelatine into ½ cup very hot water. Stir well to dissolve.

2 Beat the egg whites until softly peaking. Still beating, add the condensed milk, the cream, and the coconut milk. Add the melted gelatine, ensuring a smooth consistency. At the end, add the coconut.

3 Pour the mixture into a china bowl. Chill until it is needed.

4 For the sauce, in a small saucepan, put ¾ cup water, the prunes, and the sugar. Bring to a boil, lower the heat, and let simmer for a while. When you think that the prunes are a little softer, set aside a few whole prunes for decorating, then simmer the rest a bit more until soft. Set aside and let cool until just warm.

5 Serve the chilled manjar with warm prune sauce on top. Decorate with the reserved whole prunes.

Coconut Pudding

Quindim ou Quindão

Quindims are small tartlets widely available in Brazilian pastry shops. When we are making them at home, we tend to make slightly larger individual tarts or one big pudding because this is less fiddly. This is a very rich dish, so it is best to serve it after a light main course.

Serves 8–10 or makes
about 16 tarts

Preparation time:
15 minutes

Cooking time: 50 minutes

⋄ Generous 2½ cups

superfine sugar
⋄ 15 "thin" whites (the
thin white near the egg
yolk)
⋄ 1 Tbsp butter
⋄ Grated flesh and water
of 1 large coconut
⋄ A pinch of ground cloves

1 Preheat a 350°F oven. Beat all the ingredients together in a blender or food processor.

2 Butter a round cake tin with a hole in the middle. Dust with sugar. Pour in the pudding mixture.

3 Half-fill a large deep roasting pan with hot water. Place the tube mold or quiche pans in the water and bake in the oven for about 40 minutes. The top of the individual puddings should be brown and firm. Check if the pudding cooked in the tube mold is done by inserting a wooden toothpick into the center. If it comes out clean, this means that the pudding is ready to remove from the oven.

4 Let cool in the mold or pans for 10 minutes, then run a knife around the edge of the pudding and turn out onto baking parchment.

5 Serve at room temperature or chill until required.

Burnt Coconut Sweets

Doce de Coco Queimado

Sweets like this and many others are a common sight in the streets of Bahia. Every Bahian "tabuleiro"—"table of specialties"—will have a "doce de coco queimado," "quindims," and many, many others.

Makes around 10–12 sweets

Preparation time:
10 minutes

Cooking time: 20 minutes

⋄ 9 oz shredded coconut
⋄ ¾ tsp cinnamon
⋄ Pinch of ground cloves
⋄ 9 oz dark brown sugar
⋄ 2 egg whites

1 Mix the coconut with the ground cinnamon and the cloves.

2 Melt the sugar in a saucepan over a medium heat. Stir constantly so the sugar does not burn too much. It should become dark brown. Add the coconut and cook over low heat for 10 minutes. Keep on stirring so that the mixture does not stick to the pan. Remove from heat, let it cool, and reserve.

3 Beat the egg whites until frothy. Fold the egg whites into the pan.

4 Using two metal spoons, scoop little portions out of the pan and place them onto a baking sheet. Leave some distance between them, as the portions will run to the sides.

5 Let them cool well and they are ready to eat.

Avocado Cream
Creme de Abacate

Brazilians tend to eat avocados more as a dessert than a savory. They are often surprised when they realize that this fruit can be used in salads and savory dishes. In the same way, other nationals are often surprised to see avocados in desserts or ice cream. I assure you, they are worth a try. This is a delicious recipe and very easy to make, a favorite among Brazilian children.

Serves 4–6

Preparation time:
10 minutes
Chilling time: 30 minutes

⬦ 3 ripe avocados peeled, pitted, and cut in pieces

⬦ 1 cup fresh orange juice or 3 freshly squeezed oranges
⬦ Juice of 1 lime
⬦ 2 Tbsp granulated sugar

1 Simply put all the ingredients into a blender or food processor and mix to a smooth cream consistency.

2 Place in a suitable serving dish and chill for 30 minutes before serving.

TIP

This dessert lasts up to three days if kept in the refrigerator. If you notice a fine, dark brown layer on top, simply stir with a spoon. It does not mean that your dessert is off; the lime juice keeps it fresh.

Coconut Sweets

—— Cocada ——

These sweets can be found in nearly every Bahian street.

Makes about 10 small coconut cakes

Preparation time: 10 minutes

Cooking time: 30 minutes

- ⬦ **1 large fresh coconut**
- ⬦ **Generous 2½ cups granulated sugar**

1 Remove the coconut flesh and shred it coarsely using a hand-held shredder.

2 Place 2 cups water and the sugar in a small saucepan. Bring to a boil, lower to medium heat, and then cook until the consistency is thick and syrupy. Remove from the heat.

3 Put the coconut into a mixing bowl. Add the syrup to it and, with a wooden spoon, beat vigorously so the syrup becomes very white. Keep on beating until cool.

4 Put little portions of cocada on a baking sheet dusted with sugar and flatten each one with a fork, shaping it into a little parcel.

Pumpkin with Shredded Fresh Coconut

Doce de Abóbora com Coco

In Brazil there are several varieties of pumpkin. We hardly use the "Halloween pumpkin," although we may use one of the same shape, but much more dark orange in color. Ideally you should try to use a West Indian pumpkin. We favor a kind that resembles a large zucchini.

Serves 6–8

Preparation time:
15 minutes
Cooking time:
40–50 minutes

- ◇ 1 fresh coconut
- ◇ 1 ripe pumpkin
- ◇ Granulated sugar
- ◇ Cloves
- ◇ Cinnamon sticks

1 Remove the flesh from the coconut and shred using a hand-held shredder.

2 Peel the pumpkin, cut in small pieces, and weight it. Measure the same amount of sugar and reserve.

3 Place the pumpkin in a large saucepan, with only a third of the total volume in water. Cook until tender. Reserve a third of the water, and mash or blend the pumpkin.

4 Put the mashed pumpkin back into the saucepan, add the sugar, coconut, cloves, and cinnamon. Cook over low heat, always stirring with a wooden spoon, until the mixture starts to come away from the saucepan edges and you are able to see the base of the pan.

5 Allow to cool, then transfer to a serving dish.

Right: Pumpkin with Shredded Fresh Coconut

Coconut Custard

Baba de Moça

This traditional dessert is very sweet. Prepared using only egg yolks, this is a good way of using up your leftovers when preparing Meringue Soufflé (see page 120). It goes well with this dessert.

Serves 6

Preparation time:
15 minutes
Cooking time: 20 minutes

- ◇ 4 egg yolks
- ◇ ½ cup sugar
- ◇ 1¼ cups thick coconut milk
- ◇ ½ tsp vanilla extract

1 Put the sugar into a saucepan together with 1½ tablespoons water. Stir over a very low heat until dissolved, then add the coconut milk to the pan.

2 Pass the egg yolks through a nonmetallic strainer. Stir them with a wooden spoon, but don't beat. Remove the saucepan from the heat and add the yolks.

3 Return to low–medium heat and keep on stirring until the sauce reaches the consistency of custard. Remove from the heat and stir in vanilla.

Three-layered Pudding
Montanha Russa

Montanha Russa in Portuguese means Roller Coaster. This is possibly because when you taste this dessert you won't be able to stop eating. Serve in a glass compote jar to show it off to its best advantage.

Serves 4–6

Preparation time:
20 minutes
Cooking time: 20 minutes
Chilling time: 1 hour

TIP

To make vanilla sugar, simply insert a vanilla bean into a jar of sugar. The vanilla will give the sugar a wonderful flavor and aroma, making it ideal for use in baking and desserts.

- 4 Tbsp cornstarch
- 4 cups milk
- 1 tsp vanilla sugar
- 4 Tbsp sugar
- 8 eggs, separated
- Scant 1 cup ready-to-eat prunes, pitted
- ⅔ cup granulated sugar
- 2 small cinnamon sticks
- ¾ cup port
- Scant 1 cup superfine sugar

1 Dissolve the cornstarch in ½ cup of the milk. Put the rest of the milk in a saucepan, with the vanilla sugar and 4 tablespoons sugar. Warm over medium heat.

2 Whisk the egg yolks, then add to the saucepan, stirring. Continue to stir as you add the dissolved cornstarch. When the mixture reaches a cream consistency, turn off the heat.

3 In a small saucepan, place the prunes, granulated sugar, the cinnamon sticks, port, and a generous ½ cup water. Bring to a boil, then cook until reduced, mashing the prunes from time to time. When soft, turn off heat.

4 When both mixtures are cool, layer in a glass serving dish so you can see layers.

5 Beat the egg whites until stiffly peaking. Then beat in the superfine sugar. Using a large metal spoon, arrange the meringue on top of the bowl in small peaks. Chill and let cool for one hour before serving.

Above: The spirit of the carnival in the street at Olinda, Northeast Brazil.

Coffee Ice Cream
Sorvete de Café

No Brazilian cookery book is complete without a version of coffee ice cream. It is worth making two amounts of this recipe and keeping one in the freezer.

Serves 4

Preparation time: 40 minutes
Cooking time: 5 minutes
Freezing time: 8 hours

- 1½ cups milk, scalded
- 4 Tbsp ground strong coffee
- 4 egg yolks
- ½ cup sugar
- ¾ cup heavy cream
- ¼ tsp ground cinnamon

1 Combine the milk and ground coffee in a pan. Place over low heat, for around 10 minutes. Place a cheesecloth inside a strainer and strain the milk into a bowl. Reserve.

2 Whisk egg yolk until pale-yellow. Add sugar by degrees, still beating. Carry on beating until the mixture is light and pale. Slowly, start pouring in the milk. Then add the cream in the same way. Stir in the cinnamon.

3 Pour the mixture into a saucepan. Cook over low heat, stirring with a wooden spoon, until it has doubled in volume, about 2 or 3 minutes. Remove from heat.

4 Pour the mix into a suitable container and let cool down. Freeze it for at least 8 hours.

Passionfruit Tart
Torta de Maracujá

This tart is very simple to make. The passionfruit gives it a surprise element since tarts like this one are normally filled with apples, strawberry, or apricots.

Serves 6–8

Preparation time:
40 minutes
Cooking time: 20 minutes

For the pastry
- 2½ cups flour
- ½ cup sugar

- 2 sticks sweet butter, cubed
- 2 egg yolks

For the filling
- 6 passionfruit
- 4 Tbsp cornstarch
- ½ cup sugar

1 Preheat a 400°F oven. Sift flour and sugar together in a mixing bowl. Make a well and add butter and egg yolks. Blend with fingers to form a dough.

2 Roll out the pastry on a floured surface and use to line an 8-inch loose-bottomed flan/quiche tin. Prick with a fork then bake in the oven for 20 minutes.

3 Scoop out the pulp and seeds of the passionfruit. Blend in a blender or food processor with 1 cup water. Strain to remove ground seeds. Reserve seeds.

4 Pour this juice into a saucepan, dissolve cornstarch into it, and add sugar. Place over very low heat and, always stirring, cook until the sauce starts to thicken.

5 Rinse the reserved passionfruit seeds, then dry them in a small frying pan over very low heat, stirring with a wooden spoon. Remove from the heat and set aside.

6 When the pastry shell has cooled a little, pour in the filling and scatter the seeds over. Serve the tart chilled or at room temperature.

Cream of Eggs and Milk
Ambrosia

In the south of Brazil ambrosia is traditionally served after a barbecue, providing a contrast to a very salty main course. In the northeast, ambrosia is very welcome with Coconut Sweets (see page 103).

Serves 6

Preparation time:
15 minutes
Cooking time: 45 minutes

- 4 cups milk
- 2½ cups sugar
- 8–12 egg yolks
- 3 egg whites
- Juice of 1 small lime
- 2 cloves

1 In a large saucepan, heat up the milk and bring to a boil. Remove from the heat, add the sugar, and stir well.

2 Whisk the egg yolks and the whites together. Then gently whisk the eggs into the saucepan, little by little. Add lime juice and cloves.

3 Put the saucepan back over a low heat for 45 minutes, first stirring every 10 minutes and constantly at the end.

4 When thicker than a custard, remove from the heat. Chill for 1 hour before serving.

Right: Passionfruit Tart

Layered Cookie Tart
Pavê

*Another very rich, sweet dessert, this recipe is very popular everywhere in
Brazil and very easy to make, once you have prepared the topping in advance. The topping
can be made in two different ways. The modern, versatile Brazilians use condensed milk. I decided to
provide the old-fashioned way of making the topping. For the cookies, any kind of milk cookie will
do, but Spanish and Portuguese delicatessens sell "Maria" cookies. If you cannot find milk
cookies use Italian sweet cookies instead.*

Serves 4–6

**Preparation time:
30 minutes
Cooking time: 1 hour 20
minutes**

For the topping
- 2¼ cups milk
- ⅞ cup sugar
- 1-inch piece vanilla bean
- 1 cinnamon stick
- Shredded rind of ½ lime
- ½ cup unsalted cashews
- ½ cup sugar

For the filling
- 7 oz milk cookies
- 1 cup milk
- 7 Tbsp sugar
- 1¾ sticks butter
- 4 egg yolks
- ¾ cup heavy cream

> **TIP**
>
> *The easiest way of preparing
> the topping is putting one
> 14 oz can of condensed milk
> to boil in a saucepan with
> water. Remove the label, put
> the tin in, cover well with
> water, and boil for 1 hour.
> Let it cool to room
> temperature before opening
> or you might be badly
> burned.*

1 Ideally, you should prepare the topping a day in advance. Combine the first five ingredients in a heavy saucepan and cook over very low heat for around 45 to 50 minutes, or until the consistency is thick and firm. Remove the vanilla bean and the cinnamon.

2 To caramelize the cashews, put the nuts and the ½ cup sugar in a small saucepan. Stir constantly over low heat so the melting sugar and the nuts mix together. When the sugar is becoming dark brown, remove from heat and carefully spread the mixture over a flat buttered surface. Let cool and harden, then break it into pieces with a knife handle and set aside.

3 For the filling, soak the cookies in the milk.

4 Use a hand-held mixer to beat the sugar and the butter until pale yellow and frothy. Add the yolks and the cream.

5 In a flat, glass serving dish, alternate layers of milk-soaked cookies with layers of cream. Repeat the procedure until you get to the top of the dish, or until the cookies are used up.

6 Using a spatula, spread the topping evenly over the cookies, scatter the cashews over, and chill for an hour before serving.

Cream of Egg Yolks with Brandy
Doce de Ovos

This is a very rich but delicious recipe, another dish with Portuguese origins.
It is good to do with Meringue Soufflé (see page 120), because you can use up your spare egg yolks.
The illustration shows a runny consistency, but you can make it thicker if you wish by increasing the
cooking time a little further.

Serves 6

Preparation time:
10 minutes
Cooking time:
15–25 minutes

◇ 1¼ cups sugar
◇ 8 egg yolks
◇ ½ Tbsp salted butter
◇ 2 tsp brandy

1 Place the sugar in a saucepan with 1⅔ cups water and bring to a boil over medium heat. When boiling, dip a slotted spoon into the pan and pull out again, sideways. The sugary water will run to the bottom edge of the spoon, falling into the pan, more thickly, dripping but not hardening. Let it boil a bit more. As it boils, it will become thicker. Repeat the operation. If the liquid now hangs down from the spoon, rather than dripping finely, you have the consistency you will need for this dessert. Remove from heat and add the butter. Let it cool for 10 minutes before adding the yolks.

2 Put the yolks into a small bowl and stir gently. Strain them into the syrup with the brandy, stirring. Cook over medium–low heat until thick.

3 Let cool for 10 minutes, then pour portions into small egg cups.

TIP

This dessert also makes a delicious filling for cakes and pastries.

Above: Colorful carnival clowns in Northeast Brazil.

Chocolate Kisses
Brigadeiro

*Brigadeiros are a trademark of Brazil. Everyone knows how to make them.
I've researched, but could not find a recipe predating the advent of condensed milk. But they
are so Brazilian that I decided to include them.*

Makes about 30 little balls

Preparation time:
10 minutes
Cooking time: 35 minutes

- ½ **stick sweet butter**
- **1 14 oz can sweetened condensed milk**

- ¼ **cup milk**
- **5 Tbsp cocoa powder**
- **Colored vermicelli for rolling**

TIP

You can also use this recipe to spread over cakes. It makes a rich and delicious topping.

1 In a small saucepan, melt the butter. Add the condensed milk, the ordinary milk, and the cocoa. Stir constantly until the mixture reaches a thick consistency. Then remove from the heat and let cool.

2 Spread the colored vermicelli on a plate. Butter your hands well. With a teaspoon, scoop out little portions of the mixture, the size of an olive, and roll into a ball. Roll them in the colored vermicelli, and place in individual paper confectionery cups.

Little Coconut Kisses
Beijinhos de Coco

These are another Brazilian favorite—easily made and even more easily eaten!

Makes about 30 little balls

Preparation time:
10 minutes
Cooking time: 35 minutes

- ½ **stick sweet butter**
- 1⅔ **cups sweetened condensed milk**
- ¾ **cup freshly shredded coconut**
- ½ **cup confectioners' sugar**
- **About 30 small cloves**

1 In a small saucepan, melt the butter. Add the condensed milk and stir constantly until the mixture reaches a thick consistency. Remove from heat, wait 5 to 10 minutes, and add the coconut. Let cool.

2 Sift the sugar onto a plate. Butter your hands well. With a teaspoon, scoop out little portions of the mixture, the size of an olive, and roll into a ball. Roll them in the sugar and place them in individual paper confectionery cups. Pierce each one of them with a small clove.

Chocolate and Coconut Cake
Bolo Prestígio da Liliana

This recipe is from a friend of mine who specializes in making and improving her own recipes.
Prestígio is a Brazilian chocolate bar, filled with coconut cream!

Serves 6–8

Preparation time:
30 minutes
Cooking time:
30–40 minutes

- 4 egg yolks
- 3 Tbsp butter
- 1½ cups sugar
- ½ cup milk
- 1 tsp vanilla extract
- 2 cups flour, sifted
- 1 cup cocoa powder, sifted
- 1½ Tbsp baking powder
- 4 egg whites, beaten to a stiff peak

For the filling
- 7 oz sweetened condensed milk
- ¾ cup milk
- 5 cups shredded coconut

For the topping
- 7 oz sweetened condensed milk
- ½ cup milk
- 3 Tbsp cocoa powder
- ½ Tbsp butter

1 Preheat a 375°F oven. Beat together the yolks, butter, and sugar. Add the milk and vanilla. Add the flour and cocoa, and beat for 5 minutes more. Add the baking powder and fold in the egg whites.

2 Pour the cake mixture into a 12-inch cake pan and bake in oven for 25 to 30 minutes.

3 For the filling, put all the ingredients into a saucepan and cook over low heat for 3 minutes, always stirring, until mixture comes away from the edges of the pan.

4 Use the same method for the topping.

5 When the cake is baked, remove from the pan and let cool on a wire rack. When cool, cut the cake in half horizontally. Spread the filling over the bottom half, replace the top half, and then spread the topping over. Decorate with extra coconut scattered on top.

Coffee Cake
Bolo de Café

This is a delicious cake to be served at tea time or for breakfast.

Serves 6–8

Preparation time:
20 minutes
Cooking time: 1½ hours

- 1 cup strong coffee
- 2 eggs, lightly beaten
- 1 cup sugar
- 3 cups flour, sifted
- 1½ cups honey
- 1 Tbsp butter, at room temperature
- Generous 1 cup raisins
- 4½ oz semisweet chocolate, shredded
- 1 tsp ground cinnamon
- 1 Tbsp baking powder

1 Preheat a 350°F oven. Mix all the ingredients, except the baking powder, in a blender or food processor.

2 Add the baking powder at the very end, but make sure you mix it in well.

3 Pour the mixture into a well-buttered, 10–12-inch cake pan and bake for 1½ hours.

4 Let it cool and turn onto a plate or cooling rack.

Mango Mousse
Mousse de Manga

For this recipe look for very ripe and soft mangoes during the summer season. It is much healthier than a chocolate mousse and very simple to prepare.

Serves 4–6

Preparation time:
20 minutes
Chilling time: 60 minutes

- 6 egg yolks
- 5 Tbsp sugar
- 1 Tbsp butter at room temperature
- 2 ripe mangoes, peeled, pitted, and puréed
- 1 tsp vanilla extract
- 6 egg whites, beaten to a stiff peak

TIP
You shouldn't need to add any water to the mangoes. If the purée is too thick, just add a teaspoon at a time.

1 Beat the egg yolks with the sugar and the butter, until the mixture becomes pale.

2 Add the mango purée and the vanilla, and beat for 1 minute more

3 Fold in the egg whites. Then chill for at least 1 hour before serving.

Corn Cake

Bolo de Fubá de Sinhá

Sinhá was the name used by the slaves for the mistress of the house, probably short for senhora. This is an ancient recipe from my granny's book of delicious cakes. Unfortunately, this recipe is not suited to blenders, food processors, or even hand-held mixers, so you will have to beat it by hand (not the egg whites!).

Serves 8

Preparation time: 20 minutes

Cooking time: 30–35 minutes

- 4½ cups fine corn flour (fubá)
- 2 Tbsp flour
- 4 cups full-fat milk
- Juice of 1 lime or lemon
- 4 egg yolks
- 2 Tbsp butter
- 2 Tbsp shortening
- 2 cups sugar
- 1 Tbsp baking powder
- 1 tsp aniseed
- 7 egg whites, beaten to peaks
- Confectioners' sugar, sifted, for dusting

1 Preheat a 375°F oven. Sift together the two flours, and set aside.

2 Heat the milk over medium heat. Add the lime or lemon juice. This will make the milk separate. When it boils, take off the heat.

3 Now make a well in the center of the flour in the mixing bowl. Pour the milk into the well, little by little, always stirring with a wooden spoon.

4 Add the egg yolks, the fat, and the sugar. Keep on beating with the wooden spoon. Corn flour is heavier than all-purpose flour, so you must beat well to keep the cake light and airy.

5 When these ingredients are well mixed, add the baking powder and the aniseed. The last thing to go in is the egg whites. Fold them in gently.

6 Pour the cake mixture into a well-buttered 12-inch cake pan and bake for 30 to 35 minutes. Turn on to a plate or cooking rack. When ready to serve, dust with confectioners' sugar.

Above: Doorway detail, Ouro Prêto, Southeast Brazil.

Meringue Soufflé
Pudim de Claras

This is one of the most delicious Brazilian desserts.

Serves 6–8

Preparation time:
30 minutes
Cooking time: 20 minutes
Chilling time: 2 hours

- ½ **cup sugar**
- 10 **egg whites**
- ⅔ **cup sugar**
- ½ **tsp shredded lime**
  rind

> **TIP**
> *Warm up the egg whites in a small bowl held or placed over hot water. This will improve the consistency of the meringue.*

For the cream topping
- 1 **cup milk**
- 1 **cup thick coconut milk**
- 2 **Tbsp sugar**
- 1 **Tbsp cornstarch**
- 2 **egg yolks**
- ½ **tsp vanilla extract**
- 1 **tsp margarine**

1 Preheat a 450°F oven. In a saucepan, melt the ½ cup sugar over very low heat, stirring constantly so it does not burn. Take the saucepan off the heat and add 1½ tablespoons water. With a brush, spread the caramel around a tube pan. Alternatively, warm up your tube pan and pour the hot caramel into it. Swirl it around the mold gently. When the inner surfaces are caramelized, place the mold briefly in cold water to harden the caramel. Set aside.

2 Beat the egg whites with a hand-held mixer. While beating, little by little add the ⅔ cup sugar and the lime rind. Pour the meringue into the tube pan and bake in the oven for 10 minutes. Do not position the pan too near the top of the oven. Then let cool.

3 Run a knife around the edges of the tube pan, place a plate on top, and invert. Place a long glass upside-down in the middle of the meringue, cover with plastic wrap, and chill for 2 hours.

4 For the cream topping, in a small saucepan, warm the cow's milk and coconut milk over medium heat with the sugar until dissolved. Dissolve the cornstarch in a little cold milk, pour into the saucepan, stirring all the time. The mixture will start to thicken. Add the egg yolks and vanilla, stirring well. Remove from the heat and add the margarine. To serve pour cream topping over the meringue.

Passionfruit Manjar
Manjar de Maracujá

This is a variation of Coconut Manjar (see page 100).

Serves 4–6

Preparation time:
15 minutes

Chilling time: 1½ hours
- 15 **passionfruit**
- 6 **Tbsp sugar**
- ¾ **cup heavy cream**
- 2 **envelopes gelatine**

1 Cut passionfruit in half and scoop out pulp. Blend in a blender or food processor with ½ cup water. Pass juice through a strainer and reserve a few seeds.

2 Put the passionfruit juice back in the blender or food processor and add the sugar and cream, and mix well.

3 Dissolve the gelatine in a little hot water and add to the mixture. Beat for 1 minute more.

4 Pour the manjar into a china bowl, scatter a few passionfruit seeds over the top, and chill for 1½ hours before serving.

Cassava Cake
Bolo de Aipim

This cake is normally served for breakfast all along the northeastern coast of Brazil. Together with Bolo de Fubá (see page 118), it makes a real treat with a cup of strong black Brazilian coffee. Cassava root has a very high water content, and makes the cake very moist and compact. Don't worry that it has collapsed when you take it out of the oven; it should only be about one inch deep!

Serves 5–6

Preparation time: 30 minutes

Cooking time: 35 minutes

TIP

There are various kinds of cassava root (which is also called manioc by some people), although all resemble a large parsnip in shape, and have quite thick skin. Some are sweeter than others; some are more fibrous. In Brazil, we experiment to find the sort that suits us. Outside Brazil, I choose smaller roots with thinner, amber-colored skin.

⋄ 1 lb 2 oz cassava root
⋄ 1½ sticks butter
⋄ 2 cups sugar
⋄ A pinch of salt
⋄ 2 egg yolks
⋄ ¾ cup thick coconut milk, plus extra for brushing

1 Preheat a 375°F oven. Peel the cassava root and shred by hand or, easier, in a food processor. Set aside.

2 Using a hand-held mixer, beat together the butter, sugar, and salt until smooth and pale, then add the egg yolks and the coconut milk.

3 Using a wooden spoon, stir in shredded cassava root.

4 Spread the mixture in a 16-inch square or rectangular cake pan. Bake for about 30 minutes, until the top is golden brown and a wooden toothpick inserted in the center of the cake comes out clean. Brush the top with extra coconut milk once or twice during cooking.

5 Let cool in the pan, then cut into diamond shapes.

Drinks

Swedish-style Lime Juice

Guarana Drink

Caipirinha

Passionfruit Caipirinha, Caipiroska, and Caipiríssima

Spiced Mulled Cachaça

Cachaça Cocktail

Swedish-style Lime Juice
Limonada Suiça

Brazilians are used to a great variety of fruit juices. Some are exquisite like cashew apple (the fruit part of the cashew fruit). But the general rule is to combine and see if you like the result: try oranges and melon, pineapple and beet, papaya and milk, and watermelon and apple. This recipe is very refreshing, so try it on a hot summer's day.

Makes 1 serving

- 1 lime, ends trimmed and quartered
- 1½ Tbsp superfine sugar
- ¾ cup water
- Ice cubes

1 Put the lime quarters in a blender or food processor with the sugar and water. Blend well.

2 Add the ice cubes and blend on pulse mode. Drink immediately.

Guarana Drink
Guaraná

Guaraná is becoming very famous. It has similarities with coffee, due to the presence of a substance called guaraína (which is similar to caffeine). In Brazil, there is a fizzy drink made with guaraná, a refreshment drunk by the young and old that has no stimulating effect. Guarana powder is very bitter and rather unpleasant if drunk with water. However, there is a better way to take it, especially in the morning.

Makes 2 servings

Preparation time: 5 minutes

- 1 tsp guarana powder
- Generous 1 cup unsweetened yogurt
- 1 banana or papaya
- 1 Tbsp clear honey
- A little milk or soya milk

1 Blend the first four ingredients together.

2 Add milk or soya milk according to the consistency you like.

Above: A riot of color—Carnival, Olinda, Northeast Brazil.

Caipirinha
Caipirinha

This is the most famous and traditional Brazilian drink. Sometimes, when I say I am Brazilian, I find that people might know very little about my country, but caipirinha is one of the things they do know about. Caipirinha is normally prepared in individual servings. Brazilians often use a special wooden mortar and pestle for preparing caipirinha. Nevertheless, if you are preparing caipirinha for a group of boozy friends, it is wise to make it in a jug, otherwise you might spend the whole night making it rather than enjoying it! If you haven't got a wooden mortar, use a normal kitchen mortar. Make sure it is clean and free from other flavors.

For 1 serving

- 1 lime, ends trimmed and quartered
- 2–3 tsp superfine sugar
- 2 Tbsp cachaça/pinga
- 2 tsp water
- Ice cubes

TIP

Caipirinha is usually drunk around the pool, at the beach, or generally outdoors in the hot sun. Be very careful when preparing or drinking caipirinha in the sun. Wash your hands well or you might get lime burn; it looks awful and takes quite a long time to fade.

1 Put the lime and the sugar into a mortar. Make sure you place the lime quarters with the flesh facing up, otherwise you get a very sour caipirinha, by extracting the oil from the lime skin. (I normally peel the lime and reserve one quarter with the skin to decorate the glass.) Crush the lime with the pestle onto the sugar, being careful that the lime juice doesn't go into your eyes.

2 Decant into a glass and add the cachaça, and stir. Add the water. Stir well. Add the ice cubes. As with any drink, a lot of ice will make it weaker.

3 Taste for sugar. Brazilian taste for caipirinha is very broad: some like it very sweet; some with less sugar. The crushed limes should remain at the bottom of the glass.

For 4–6 servings

- 6–8 limes, ends trimmed and quartered
- 4 Tbsp superfine sugar
- 1 bottle of cachaça/pinga
- Ice cubes

1 Crush the limes hard, well into the sugar using a pestle and mortar.

2 Pour the mixture into a jug, add the cachaça, and stir. Add the ice cubes. Water is optional in this version, since the ice cubes will gradually melt in the jug.

Passionfruit Caipirinha

—— Caipirinha de Maracujá ——

This is a variation of caipirinha. Brazilians these days experiment with all sorts of fruits.
You could try with kiwi fruit too.

For 1 serving

- 1 passionfruit
- 2 tsp superfine sugar
- 3–4 ½ Tbsp cachaça/pinga
- 2 tsp water
- Ice cubes

For 4–6 servings

- 6–8 passionfruit
- 4 Tbsp superfine sugar
- 1 bottle cachaça/pinga
- Ice cubes

> **TIP**
>
> *You might strain the mixture, to get rid of the seeds, but they look quite attractive at the bottom of the glass.*

1 Cut the passionfruit in half. Scoop the pulp into a thick glass, and add the sugar. Mix these together well.

2 Add the cachaça. Taste for sugar. Add the water. Stir well. Add ice cubes.

Variations

Caipiroska
Caipiroska is caipirinha made with vodka. To make caipiroska, substitute vodka for the cachaça.

Caipiríssima
Caipiríssima is caipirinha made with white rum. To make caipiríssima, substitute white rum for the cachaça.

Spiced Mulled Cachaça

—— Quentão com Cachaça ——

Quentão is a traditional drink of São Paulo state. From São Paulo down to the south of
the country, Brazilians can claim a winter season, since from Rio up to the northeastern states,
the average winter temperature is 73°F. Quentão is served warm.

Makes 4–6 servings

Preparation time:
10 minutes
Cooking time: 10 minutes

- 2 cups superfine sugar
- Scant ½ cup water

- 2 limes, sliced fine
- 3-in piece fresh ginger root, cubed
- ½ a whole nutmeg
- 3 cinnamon sticks
- 4 cloves
- 1 bottle of cachaça or white rum

1 In a saucepan, burn the sugar until light brown. Add the water, sliced limes, ginger, nutmeg, cinnamon, and cloves. Bring to a boil and simmer until thick but liquid.

2 Turn off the heat. Add the cachaça. Stir well.

3 Warm through before serving. You may place it in a bain-marie to keep warm.

Cachaça Cocktail
Batidas

Batidas (also called porradinhas—little punches) are another alcoholic drink, very popular, especially in São Paulo and Rio de Janeiro. As with caipirinha, you can experiment with all sorts of fruit juices. Some variations are made with condensed milk instead of sugar and are much too sweet. Others are made with an egg white. This is a basic recipe and you can play around with variations, but beware of the hangover!

Makes 1 serving

Preparation time: 5 minutes

◇ ¼ cup cachaça
◇ **2 Tbsp fresh coconut milk**
◇ **2 Tbsp superfine sugar**
◇ **Ice cubes**

1 Blend everything together, including the ice.

Sources, Acknowledgements, and Picture Credits

Brazil Amazônia Store Inc.
3317 31st Avenue
Long Island City
NY 10001
Tel. 718 2041521
Fax. 718 2048108
Contact: Tânia

● All ingredients stocked

● Mail order available

Búzios
11 46th Street
2nd Floor
New York
NY 10036
Tel. 212 869 65552

● All ingredients stocked

● Mail order available

Coisa Nossa
70 Adams Street
Newark
NJ 07105
Tel. 973-5782675

● Dendê oil and malagueta pepper

**Kapox International, Inc./
Amazon Fruit Company**
45 Bell Street
Suite 3
Chagrin Falls
OH 44022
Tel. 216-247 97 00

● Best Amazonian Guraná (liquid, powder and sticks), coffee, different varieties of fruit pulps from tropical places

Lorenzo's Fruit and Vegetable
16445 W. Dixie Hwy.
North Miami
FL 33160
Tel. 305-9445052

Lorenzo's Groceries
16385 W. Dixie Hwy.
North Miami
FL 33160
Tel. 305-9456381

Salumeria Biellese
378 8th Avenue
New York
NY 10001
Tel. 212-7367376

Seabra's
60 Lafayette Street
Newark
NJ 07105
Tel. 973-589-8606

● Great variety of fruit and vegetables

● Tins and preserved ingredients, heart of palm, preserved mushrooms

● Slab bacon, chorizo, calabresa, and smoked meats

● Fruit, Cassava flour, Beans, Carne seca-dried meat, Paio, Slab bacon, Couve (kale), Palmito (heart of palm)

Acknowledgements The publishers would like to thank Lisboa Delicatessen, 54 Golborne Road, London W10, England, for their help in the preparation of this book.

Picture Credits pp 6, 7, 8, 10, 11, 12, 13, 15, 26, 30, 36, 38, 41, 43, 45, 48, 50, 52, 55, 56, 61, 68, 73, 74, 76, 79, 84, 86, 89, 90, 93, 107, 112, 118, 122, 123, 127, Peter Wilson.

Index